# OLD-FASHIONED ROSES

# OLD-FASHIONED ROSES

*Their Care and Cultivation*

AMANDA BEALES

Introduction by Peter Beales

Picture Editor Vincent Page

CASSELL

Cassell Publishers Limited
Artillery House, Artillery Row
London SW1 1RT

First published 1990

British Library Cataloguing in Publication Data

Beales, Amanda
Old-fashioned roses
1. Roses. Cultivation
I. Title
635.9'33372

ISBN 0-304-31971-6

Produced by Justin Knowles Publishing Group
9 Colleton Crescent, Exeter EX2 4BY

Editor: Roy Gasson

Line illustrations: David Ashby

Typeset by Keyspools Ltd
Printed and bound in Hong Kong

# CONTENTS

# LIST OF PLATES

# INTRODUCTION

I can remember the first time I saw a rose. It was on an old, decrepit arch in my grandmother's garden, and I can have been aged only three or four. I remember it had a perfume and thorns and that it was pink with lots and lots of flowers, but my memory of its shape and form is hazy. I have never returned to that garden – indeed, I doubt if it is there now, because the old house has been rebuilt – but I feel sure that the rose must have been 'Dorothy Perkins'. A few years later, in the garden of my other grandparents, I found 'Maiden's Blush'. That rose is still there, exactly as I remember it, thriving. 'Maiden's Blush' is still one of my favourites. Another pet of mine is the simple dog rose, I suppose because I remember its profusion in the hedgerows of rural Norfolk on my way to and from school. Suckering was one of the first jobs I learned as an apprentice rose grower. Later, when proved to be trustworthy under a hard taskmaster, I learned budding. The thrill of joining two plants together soon wore off – I found it too repetitive and wangled my way into other jobs that took me into closer contact with more mature plants. Most of the roses I got to know in those days were Hybrid Teas and the Hybrid Polyanthas, which were later renamed Floribundas. There were ever-changing fashions for roses – the most modern and up-to-date were always in biggest demand and, as is the case now with modern roses, they were usually the brightest and most flamboyant. I, too, fell for the brightest colours and rather ignored the older roses that I have now come to enjoy most of all.

I first learned to appreciate the more subtle shades of the old roses when fetching and carrying blooms of such varieties as 'Tuscany Superb' and 'Belle de Crécy' for my boss and mentor Edward LeGrice as he went about his work of breeding in search of new varieties. Of all my apprenticeship tasks, acting as hybridizer's assistant was the one I most enjoyed. It was while doing this that I learned to recognize and identify more and more varieties, finding the mystery of hybridizing very rewarding.

At the time I worked for Edward LeGrice he was undisputed leader in the breeding of Floribundas, at least in Britain, following on from the foundations laid by Poulsen of Denmark in the 1920s and '30s. To achieve his colour breaks, he cleverly crossed the best of the new with the best of the old, realizing that, by and large, breeders of the day, creditable though their achievements were, had somehow lost their way in their search for continuity of flower and brighter and brighter colours, leaving behind for ever, it was then thought, the quieter colours and exquisite shapes of yesterday's roses, considered unwanted by the great general public. Looking through old catalogues, I shudder to see names of roses then widely grown that fell into oblivion and extinction during the 1930s, '40s, and '50s, at the expense of relative rubbish introduced as novelties.

Fortunately though, despite being dropped from catalogues, many of the old varieties, by virtue of their strong constitutions, were still around – often unlabelled and often in unkempt gardens. Also, one or two good collections of roses remained in various parts of the world and, just in time, a few enlightened plantsmen and rosarians realized that, unless they were preserved, many old varieties were in danger of disappearing for ever. One of the most active of these was Graham Stuart Thomas, who had over the years sought out and put together a large collection of rarities. Quite apart from collecting, Thomas had made a careful, scholarly study of them, imparting this knowledge in his classic book, *The Old Shrub Roses*, rekindling interest in them and proving that the public had not been totally taken in by the ever-increasing numbers of modern roses coming on to the market. Their revival continued, gaining momentum through the 1960s, '70s, and '80s. Now there is much world-wide interest in their preservation, their future is secure, and demand seems almost insatiable.

Up until a few years ago I thought of Britain, and England in particular, as the home of the rose, but while this may have been true in Victorian and Edwardian times it most certainly is not the case today. In the United States, for example, heritage rose enthusiasts have formed themselves into groups and sub-groups dedicated to the preservation, and the dissemination of wider knowledge, of the older varieties. The same applies in many other countries where roses grow well. On a recent visit, I found several collections and many dedicated enthusiasts in both Australia and New Zealand. Naturally, as interest in their preservation has increased, so more and more beautiful old varieties have been discovered. Authenticating these has been, and is, a problem, but what is more important is that they have not been lost.

One small but enthusiastic group of heritage rose lovers came together on the island of Bermuda in 1956 to preserve the many mysterious rose varieties that were to be found there – taken from Europe and the United States during the 19th century. Most are either Chinas or Teas. Both types found soil and temperatures to their liking and as a result outlived their counterparts growing in less congenial climates elsewhere. Also Bermuda, unlike larger centres of population had until recently no rose breeders or rose nurseries. Consequently distribution has been largely from cuttings handed around among gardening friends and the island has been isolated from the pressures of a constant influx of new varieties.

What is it that makes the older roses so captivat-

ing? Is it their history, their aura of mystery and romance, their unrivalled beauty of form, their perfume, their sheer range, or, simply, their names? To me, it is all these things plus their versatility in coping with almost any landscaping problem in almost any garden, large or small, ancient or modern.

If it is their history that endears the older roses to so many people then I understand for, in my case, knowing that a rose was grown by gardeners, in China, Persia, or Rome, before civilization came properly to northern Europe, is a very good reason for me to grow it too. Equally rewarding is the knowledge that my own Victorian ancestors were perhaps tending and enjoying the same varieties that I now grow and love. It is fascinating to me, too, to realize that in prehistoric times the distribution of the genus was entirely confined to the northern hemisphere and yet, nowadays, descendants of these species are growing happily south of the equator. Why? Is it simply that they did grow in the south but that we have so far found no fossilized evidence of their existence, or is it that roses in those far-off days had no part in the balance of nature except in the north? More likely, with roses being confined to temperate regions, there were no natural means by which they could make their way south through the tropics until man started to travel and to carry them or their seeds with him.

Far and away the majority of species have their origins in Asia and the Orient and, it is from these, and from *Rosa chinensis* in particular, that modern roses have inherited their long-flowering capability. *R. multiflora* also came to Europe from the East and, without the genes from this species, none of today's taken-for-granted cluster-flowered varieties could exist. This makes it sound as though our native European roses had no part to play in the development of modern varieties, but this is not so – from these have come much of the perfume and most of the hardiness required to grow roses north of the 45th parallel.

Although species roses are of less interest to some lovers of old roses, I find them fascinating, both botanically and as garden plants. Among their ranks are dwarves and giants and although, by and large, they have a relatively short flowering season, it is no shorter than many other flowering shrubs and quite a few offer much more than just flowers, in the form of hips and foliage. If more modern landscapers would think of them in terms of flowering shrubs instead of as roses, perhaps more would find their way into our parks and gardens.

We do not know when man first took to interfering in the natural lineage of the rose and began to cross one with another to create hybrids. At first, rose breeding would have been haphazard – although pollen may have been transferred from one to another, this was probably achieved more by close proximity planting than by fertilization by hand. In fact, right up to the time of Henry Bennett in the late 19th century, it was the practice of raisers simply to gather seeds at random and germinate these to see what came up, selecting the best for naming and introduction.

My favourite period of rose history is the late 18th and early 19th centuries, at the time of the Empress Josephine. Josephine, it is said, collected over one hundred and fifty varieties of Gallicas, and although many may have been far from true to type, I would dearly love to have seen them. It was during that period too that the main influence of the stud China roses was felt, in that the Portlands, Bourbons, and Noisettes were born in different parts of the world and, slightly later, the Hybrid Perpetuals.

Partly because of the climate in the south of France and partly from the influence of the Empress Josephine through her patronage of rose growers, the French led the world in rose breeding throughout the best part of the 19th century. Indeed, it was a Frenchman, Jean-Baptiste Guillot, who, in 1867, introduced 'La France', reputed to be the first Hybrid Tea and, eight years later, 'Pâquerette', the first Polyantha, both important milestones in the development of modern roses. Later, in 1898, another Frenchman, Joseph Pernet-Ducher, after much work and many false starts, introduced 'Soleil d'Or', the orange-yellow rose that first brought yellow into the ranks of Hybrid Teas.

By 1890, the British, especially William Paul and Henry Bennett, were making significant progress with their introductions and by the turn of the century British breeders began to dominate, especially in the breeding of Hybrid Teas and Hybrid Perpetuals. Another landmark came in 1913 when the Rev. Joseph Pemberton started to introduce his cluster-flowered shrubs, to become known as Hybrid Musks, a group of roses that rank among the best and most garden-worthy of all the roses from the past.

Where is the demarcation? When is a modern rose an old rose and, how is the line drawn between the two? I consider that any rose that meets certain aesthetic criteria and that is of garden value qualifies, especially if it has disappeared or is disappearing from catalogues, by virtue of becoming old-fashioned or out of date. If age alone were the yardstick, then the field is narrowed to include only the Albas, Centifolias, Gallicas, Noisettes, Bourbons, Portlands, Hybrid Perpetuals, some of the early Teas, and the Chinas, thus excluding most of the later Teas, the Hybrid Teas, and the Polyanthas. I would be the first to admit that many of the older roses of this latter group cannot perform as well as their modern counterparts, especially in freedom of flower, but even the most ardent supporter of modern varieties will admit that in shape and form, and often in scent, many of the old varieties have the edge.

This brings me to the second possible reason why old roses are so well loved – their aura of mystery and romance. These roses have a 'presence' in a garden that is impossible to define. In some ways I suppose this is because of their history, but it is also about nostalgia and sentimentality, depending on one's mood. The older the rose the more obvious is its presence. But, of course, it may all be explained by imagination. Take the Albas for example, some of the most beautiful of all roses. As plants they are unobtrusive even when in full flush but, when seen at their best, it is not difficult to imagine them in gardens of the past.

Then there is the unrivalled beauty of form of old roses. To those of us who are committed to the older roses, the true and proper shape of a rose is not that of the modern Hybrid Tea, but much flatter and shorter-petalled. The Hybrid Tea is certainly beautiful in its own way, but it is high centred and consequently made up of large petals that make it rather shapeless when fully open, especially when the flower is made up of only a few petals. But the flat, full flower is just one of the many different shapes that exist within the ranks of old roses – some of the loveliest are the singles and semi-doubles that, when open, display their stamens to advantage. The fullest and most shapely of all the older groups are the Centifolias – their very name means 'one hundred leaves', which should be interpreted as 'one hundred petals'. Another classical shape to be found among old roses is the cup. A rose with this form is usually fairly full of short petals in its centre, with longer petals around its edge to form the cup. When in bud and partially open, these roses usually have a flattish top. Two of the best known roses of this shape are the Bourbons 'La Reine Victoria' and its sport 'Mme Pierre Oger'. Quite a few other Bourbons are also cupped, a shape inherited from the China part of their ancestry, the flatter, more fully double Bourbons acquiring their shape and make-up from the Damask side of their lineage.

The reason why every garden is not full of old roses is because they cannot compete with modern varieties for quantity of flowers and many flower for only two or three weeks of the year. This I understand, for in beds and mixed borders, especially in smaller gardens, a long flowering season is important. If, though, old roses are considered as shrubs the short-flowering argument against them ceases to carry any weight, because very few flowering shrubs flower for longer than two or three weeks each year and even fewer flower in high summer at the time shrub roses are out.

Another reason why old roses are captivating is their scent. Unlike the moderns, very few are without any trace of scent. However I have always felt that general comparisons in fragrance between modern and old roses are unfair.

Up until the 1920s it seems that almost every rose introduced was fragrant to some extent, but, as the search for more freedom of flower and brighter colours gathered momentum, so fragrance became lost in many varieties. The early Floribundas, with a few exceptions, were devoid of any scent and they remained scentless right through to the mid-1970s, when several well-perfumed varieties were introduced. The Hybrid Teas too, particularly those brightly coloured varieties raised in the 1940s and '50s, also lost their perfume. Modern breeders, though, have responded well to criticism and very few, if any, scentless modern Hybrid Teas or Floribundas are now introduced.

If there is a difference between the scent of old and modern roses, it is in the quality, the older roses wearing by far the most refined and most expensive of perfumes. Finest of all is that of the Albas, light, fresh, delicate, and lingering but not overpowering. Slightly less refined and even stronger are the heady, dense fragrances of the Centifolias and Damasks.

Mention must be made of one or two special perfumes. It is said that Tea roses, when they first came from China, were so called because their fragrance resembled the aroma of freshly opened tea chests. Certainly, most Teas have a distinctive perfume, but personally I can find little resemblance to that of tea. It is more likely that, since the early Teas came to Europe as part of the cargo of the old tea clippers, the name is derived from their mode of transport rather than from their scent – or perhaps the plants themselves, when unpacked, smelled of tea. The foliage of roses of the Sweetbrier family, *Rosa eglanteria*, gives off an aroma of apples, the leaves and flowers of *R. primula* smell distinctly of incense, and the large, shaggy blooms of 'Constance Spry' have the scent of myrrh. The flowers of the beautiful Rugosa 'Roseraie de l'Hay' smell strongly of cloves and those of *R. mulliganii* have a scent reminiscent of banana. Quite a few other roses have fruity scents – 'Leverkusen' has a distinctly lemon fragrance and 'Mme Isaac Pereire' (see page 100) is thought by many to smell of raspberries. Several roses, as though to confuse the bees, copy the scent of other flowers – 'Félicité et Perpétue' (page 56) smells of primroses and *R. banksiae* 'Lutea' of violets.

Fragrance in old roses is not entirely concentrated in foliage and petals. The moss of the Moss roses is frequently aromatic, especially when touched, when the perfume from the sometimes slightly sticky moss will linger on the fingers for hours.

Another reason for choosing old roses is their sheer variety and range. Their colours range from pure white through yellow, and through blush to pale pink, to deep red, and some purple shades border almost on blue. No other plant can offer such diversity of forms, from pot plant to tree climber. Its uses in the garden are manifold.

A number of short, tidy, older roses will fit into the small garden, as open ground plants, among others in mixed borders, or as pot plants on terraces or patios. Best of all for these purposes are the Portland Damasks. These have large, full blooms that they produce regularly throughout the summer. They are mostly of pastel shades, from white to pink and soft purple. If bright colours are required then the best choice would be from the range of those delightful little roses, the Dwarf Polyanthas. Their flowers individually are rather insignificant, but they are produced in large numbers and collectively they make stunning displays. About ten varieties have come to us from earlier in this century; their colours range from white through the pinks and oranges to deep red. It would be good to see more roses grown in pots. It is not in any way difficult and there are plenty of varieties that make themselves comfortable when grown in this way, in the greenhouse or conservatory or out of doors.

By far the largest number of old-fashioned roses fall into the middle-size bracket. Among these can be found such diverse types as summer-flowering Gallicas, continuous-flowering Hybrid Musks, the sprawling Centifolias and Damasks, the tidier Albas, the sparse Bourbons, and the dense Rugosas, not to mention the lanky Hybrid Perpetuals. Their uses range from hedging, both formal and informal, to specimen planting in lawns, but most of all I like to see them used as flowering shrubs, either in mixed shrubberies or among herbaceous plants, where they give the bed that little extra height.

Quite a large number of shrub roses will grow to a height of 6ft (2m) or more, and these can sometimes outgrow their welcome in smaller gardens. If space permits, however, they can be most rewarding either as free-standing shrubs or, in the case of the lax and untidy varieties, supported on tripods or some such structure. Some of the taller, denser varieties make good ornamental hedges and many of the species roses make useful shrubs in woodlands and coverts.

So far, I have made little mention of Climbers and Ramblers, but there are so many excellent types and varieties that it is hard to know where to start. Over the years we have collected together about two hundred and fifty varieties at our nursery and most of these were introduced more than fifty years ago.

They divide roughly equally between Climbers and Ramblers and vary in size from the small Noisettes and Climbing Teas to the vigorous *Rosa filipes* 'Kiftsgate', which is capable of climbing 30ft (9m) or more into trees.

There is often confusion as to the difference between Climbers and Ramblers. Generally speaking, Climbers have larger flowers, which are produced on new wood made in the same season. Ramblers have smaller flowers, usually in clusters, which are produced on wood made in the previous season. Ramblers usually have thinnish, pliable growth, while the wood of Climbers is mostly thick and firm – although there are some notable exceptions to the rule, such as 'Mermaid', 'Mme Alfred Carrière', and 'New Dawn'. Most Climbers and Ramblers flower only once each season, although occasionally some will repeat a few flowers in the autumn. Climbers are probably best used on walls and on taller, more sturdy, rustic trellises. Ramblers, because they are so pliable, are ideal for arches and arbours.

The final possible reason for choosing old-fashioned roses is because of the mystique of their names. There can be few greater compliments than having a rose named after you, or for you. In the 19th century it was the fashion to give roses the names of famous people. Those who wished for their very own rose would let it be known to the rose breeders of the day, who would either bestow a name in gratitude for patronage, in return for a fee from a loving husband or suitor, or – occasionally, and less cynically – in honour of a dignitary whom they admired or respected. It was, also, not uncommon to change the name of a rose to commemorate an event or special occasion or to pander to royalty. This last was the case in 'Rose Lelieur', which was originally named after its raiser, Comte Lelieur, who was in charge of all the imperial gardens of France in 1815. When King Louis XVIII saw the rose he asked if it could be renamed 'Rose du Roi'. What would have happened to the Comte had he said no? An example of the power of money is seen in the naming of 'Mme Isaac Pereire'. Isaac Pereire was a banker of considerable means and influence and, when his wife first saw the Bourbon rose 'Le Bien Heureux de la Salle', she asked him to persuade the raiser, Monsieur Garcon, to rename it after her. One wonders how much it cost? Mme Pereire chose well; she has immortalized her name, for her rose is one of the most popular of the Bourbons and will, undoubtedly, remain so.

The striped Gallica Rosa Mundi is named after Fair Rosamund, mistress of Henry II, so the legend goes. It is a pleasant story, but one that, without documentary evidence, we can never prove or disprove. I like to think there is at least a grain of truth in this story, for there is little doubt in my mind that this striped sport from *R. gallica* 'Officinalis' was around at that time.

Rose catalogues from the 19th century read like pages from the social register for, during that century, very few ladies of the French royal family and aristocracy failed to have a rose named after them. Indeed, it was a Frenchman, Schwartz, who named a beautiful Bourbon after Queen Victoria.

'Charles de Mills' (page 71) is one of the loveliest of the Gallicas. It is obviously an old variety, but no one knows who Charles de Mills was. There are some mysterious women, too. I would love to know who Ghislaine de Féligonde and Zéphirine Drouhin were.

At London's Chelsea Show in 1912, the *Daily Mail* newspaper held a competition for the best new rose in the show. The prize of a gold cup and of one thousand pounds was won by the French breeder Joseph Pernet-Ducher. But a condition of winning the prize was that the rose should be named after the newspaper, and unfortunately Pernet-Ducher's rose had already been named 'Mme Edouard Herriot', after the wife of the Mayor of Lyon. Not for any amount of prize money would he change it. Edouard Herriot, who subsequently became premier of France, was a man of some influence so, after much controversy, it was agreed that the rose should retain the name of his wife in France but become known as the 'Daily Mail' in England. We must assume that Pernet-Ducher was paid his prize money in full.

These days roses are frequently used in advertising and in the marketing of many unrelated products; to this end publicity and advertising companies will pay considerable sums of money to breeders to have the names of their clients linked to them, sometimes, unfortunately, to the detriment of the rose. This practice is by no means new, however. In 1890, twenty-two years before his contretemps with the *Daily Mail*, Pernet-Ducher accepted payment from a famous Grenoble couturiere with shops in both Paris and London, in exchange for naming a rose after her. The lady chose well and the rose, 'Mme Caroline Testout', (page 68) turned out to be one of the best Hybrid Teas ever raised. In its heyday it sold by the million world-wide. Another famous rose named for advertising purposes is 'Dorothy Perkins', named after a famous American store, which gave away thousands of plants in 1902, the year of its introduction.

Having discussed the various possibilities as to why old roses are so captivating and worthwhile, it is perhaps worth speculating for a while on our modern roses. How many will still be with us in the 21st century? Not too many I suspect. And which of those will be worth preserving then as old-fashioned or heritage roses? Looking through our present-day catalogues, I suggest that about half of the modern Floribundas and Hybrid Teas will have disappeared within ten years and, at least half again within twenty and, by the year 2020 only about six or eight will still be grown – and these only by those nurseries specializing in old varieties. My forecast of six of each is as follows. Of the Hybrid Teas: 'Peace', 'Grandpa Dickson', 'Alexander', 'Silver Jubilee', 'Whisky Mac', and 'King's Ransom'. Of the Floribundas: 'Allgold', 'Iceberg', 'Mountbatten', 'Pink Parfait', 'Margaret Merril', and 'Queen Elizabeth'.

As to the future of old roses, I believe they will always be with us and I would anticipate that demand will continue to increase. However, I suspect that new methods of propagation will, eventually, be perfected and that this will result in a period of over-production that will, at first, be good for the consumer but will, eventually, result in shorter and shorter lists, for micropropagation is viable only where large numbers are produced. As for the types of roses that will be popular and in demand in, say, thirty years time, the trend, at present, shows that more and more compact and spreading roses are being bred and, since they fit perfectly into the modern, smaller garden, I expect more and more to appear in catalogues at the expense of the taller roses. Genetic engineering is still in its infancy but it may well be that future rose breeders will dispense with haphazard forecasting of results and produce new varieties to order in test tubes.

All this sounds like science fiction and I hope it is. Who wants a rose from a test tube? But when I was young I never dreamed that I would today be using a computer to do my stock control. And I had never heard of polythene bags!

Whatever the future holds, roses, and old roses in particular, will still be with us, for no amount of science can improve upon one of nature's most beautiful creations.

PETER BEALES

# THE GROUPS OF OLD-FASHIONED ROSES

## Alba Roses

This group dates from far back in time. Some of the Alba roses grown today are known to have been in existence in the 15th century.

Albas make splendid plants; they have a grace not found in any other group. Their colourings are tranquil, from white to mid-pink, and their grey leaves set off the flowers exquisitely. They all have the most pervasive perfumes. Other attributes of these roses are their tolerance of hardships such as poor soil and semi-shade and their longevity.

Some say that it is a pity that they are only summer flowering. Perhaps this is so, but even after the flowers have gone they still retain their foliage, which blends well with other plants.

## Banksiae Roses

The Banksiae roses, a family of early flowering, thornless ramblers, can, given the right position, be quite fantastic. Probably the most common and best known is *Rosa banksiae* 'Lutea'. This produces clusters of small, double, yellow flowers. Lesser known but equally rewarding are *R. b. lutescens*, with vivid yellow, slightly larger, single flowers, *R. b. normalis* (probably the true species), with single, white flowers, and *R. b. alba-plena*, a fully double white. All these do well under glass, but they will need plenty of room to expand, for they do not enjoy being hard pruned. *R. × fortuniana* is also a member of the Banksiae family. This is less vigorous, maturing at a height of about 12ft (3.5m). Its flowers are large, fully double and pure white, but never produced in great quantities.

## Bourbon Roses

The first Bourbon rose was born on the Isle de Bourbon, an island in the Indian Ocean now called Réunion. It was a chance cross between the China rose 'Parson's Pink' (now called 'Old Blush') and the Damask 'Quatre Saisons'. After discovery by a man named Brèon, it was sent to France and given the name 'Rose Edouard'. Its potential as breeding material was immediately recognized by a Monsieur Jacques who raised seedlings, one of which was given the name 'Bourbon Queen' and so another new race came about. As usual, other growers soon jumped on the bandwagon and began to raise new varieties. Many of those early Bourbons are still around today and they are as well loved as ever.

As plants the Bourbons are very variable. Some will attain heights in excess of 10ft (3m) and others remain shrubby bushes, no more than 3ft (1m) high. Most flower throughout the summer, although 'Bourbon Queen', for example, one of the most beautiful, flowers only once in early summer. In flower form, too, they vary, from the large blowsy cerise 'Mme Isaac Pereire' (page 100) to the small shapely white 'Boule de Neige'. They are invariably scented. Their uses range from specimen shrubs to pot plants and their charm is such that they will always find a prominent place in my garden, especially my favourite, 'Souvenir de la Malmaison' (page 108).

## Centifolias

Less is known about the Centifolias perhaps than any other group of roses. What is certain is that they have a complicated ancestry and that much of their evolution took place in the 15th and 16th centuries in Holland, where more than two hundred varieties were produced by breeders.

As garden plants, most are straggly and coarse but, with a little judicious pruning and perhaps support, they can be contained. They are all summer flowering only, but among their varieties are some of the most beautiful and highly scented of all the old-fashioned roses. Two worth singling out for mention are *Rosa centifolia* 'Bullata', a rose that produces huge, many-petalled flowers among large, lettuce-like leaves, and 'Rose de Meaux', a short and stocky variety that yields a profusion of small, rosette-like flowers and is ideal for the small garden or a pot.

## China Roses

These are an interesting family with origins in the country from which they take their name. Their main claim to fame is that they brought remontancy and continuity of flowers to European roses.

As garden plants, they can often be fastidious, preferring good soil and sunny situations. Nonetheless, a variety can normally be chosen to fit most situations and, in the last resort, if the garden soil is not suitable, most will grow well in tubs. Like their cousins the Teas, some do not enjoy harsh winters. The bush forms rarely exceed 4ft (1.2m) in height and they have a tendency to be a little sprawly, a habit accentuated by thin, twiggy growth and, in some cases, sparseness of foliage. However, any shortage of leaves is usually well compensated for by masses of flowers, which will continue, on most varieties, all summer long. The climbing forms are easier to grow and are usually better clothed with leaves.

With such similarity of growth habits, it is perhaps a little surprising to find that these hybrids have a wide and varied assortment of flower types, from the large, fully double flowers of the creamy-peach 'Irène Watts' to the yellow, peach, and strawberry pink combinations of the single 'Mutabilis'. 'Cécile Brunner' (page 62) is one of the best known of the Chinas and one of the most beautiful. This little rose will attain a height of about 3ft (1m) in good soil as a bush; the climbing form will reach incredible heights.

## Damask Roses

The Damasks are a very old and complicated family. They were grown in the Middle East, where they were prized for their scent and used extensively in the manufacture of perfume. It is not known exactly when they came to Europe but the Romans certainly knew and enjoyed them. Today, some are still used by perfumiers – in fact, one, 'Kazanlik', bears the name of one of the leading areas of rose-attar production in Bulgaria.

Most of the earliest Damasks were summer flowering only, but one, *Rosa damascena bifera*, known commonly as 'Quatre Saisons', gives a good flush of secondary flowers in the autumn. This rose, accidentally crossed with the China 'Old Blush', brought forth the Bourbons and also played a major role in the birth of the Portlands.

Damasks form a fairly small group – about ten are listed in specialists' catalogues. My favourite is 'Mme Hardy' (page 83), a beautiful, pure white with an exquisite perfume. As garden plants they are mostly accommodating and not difficult to grow, although they definitely have a taste for the best soils.

## Floribunda Roses

The name Floribunda was adopted in the early 1950s for what until then were called Hybrid Polyanthas. When these roses first appeared, from crosses made by the Danish breeder Poulsen between Dwarf Polyanthas and Hybrid Teas, they were known as Poulsen Roses. However, when other breeders started to introduce others in the 1930s they became Hybrid Polyanthas, quite a good name considering their pedigree. However, by the 1950s they were becoming so unlike their ancestors that the name was thought to be misleading.

Floribunda is an apt name, for floriferousness is the main attribute of these roses. Several old-fashioned roses that would originally have been introduced as Polypompons or even Polyanthas now fit snugly into this category because of their habit of producing many flowers in large clusters. More recently, the Classification Committee of the World Federation of Rose Societies have recommended a further change of name to, simply, Cluster Flowered Roses, but there has been a distinct reluctance to accept this in the trade and most nursery catalogues still list them as Floribundas.

## Gallica Roses

It is pleasant to believe, in spite of the sceptics, that there is truth in the legend that crusaders of the 12th and 13th centuries brought roses to Europe from the East and even more pleasant to think that perhaps *Rosa gallica* and the Apothecary's Rose, *R.g.* 'Officinalis' (page 111), were two of them. Certainly, the Persians had a Gallica rose as a religious emblem at least twelve hundred years before Christ.

The Empress Josephine is said to have had a collection of over one hundred and fifty varieties of Gallicas and although many of these have now been lost, we still have several from which to choose. 'Complicata' (page 73) is one of my favourites; it is one of the largest Gallicas and very beautiful when in full bloom. No one who grows old roses can be without 'Charles de Mills' (page 71), a rose that both blends and contrasts so beautifully with softer colours, as does 'Tuscany Superb' (page 58), with its deep ruby flowers and bold golden anthers. There are several striped Gallicas, the most famous of which is Rosa Mundi, *R.g.* 'Versicolor' (page 112), a sport from *R.g.* 'Officinalis', but some prefer the more double 'Camaieux'. These roses are easy to grow in all soils and will tolerate some shade. Most are well scented.

Those who insist on a repeat of flowering should not choose Gallicas, but their gardens will be the poorer without them.

## Hybrid Musk Roses

When first introduced, these roses were called Pemberton Roses, after the Rev. Joseph Pemberton, who first bred them between 1913 and 1926. His first two were 'Moonlight' (page 50) and 'Danaë', both of which remain popular to this day – as do most of his varieties. One could say that Pemberton is the father of the modern shrub rose for, until his roses came along there were no other cluster-flowered varieties of such accommodating size and continuity of flower. At first his roses were introduced as Hybrid Teas but, by the year 1920, they had been classified separately as Hybrid Musks, because of the Moschata influence in their parentage. Today they are

probably more valuable than they were then, for we have learned to use them more effectively as shrubs.

Most Hybrid Musks are Pemberton's, but after his death a few other breeders capitalized on his work with some excellent varieties. They have a wide colour range, from the soft creamy shades of 'Prosperity' (page 59) to the strong red of 'Wilhelm'. Their flower shape and size also vary widely, from the fully double 'Buff Beauty' (page 97) to the single 'Ballerina' (page 60). Most are scented, although none overpoweringly so, and all have glossy foliage on smooth, pliable wood with few thorns. They are extremely useful either in mixed borders or in beds to themselves. Some of the less sprawly varieties also make excellent hedges, but most of all I like to see them used, sparingly, among herbaceous plants.

## Hybrid Perpetual Roses

Like most of the best of the old roses, the Hybrid Perpetuals started life in the early 1800s from a mixture of crosses. Perhaps the name is slightly misleading, because they tend to be repeat flowering rather than perpetual, but the early raisers can be

Hybrid Perpetual rose

forgiven for this slight exaggeration because among them are some real beauties. They were the forerunners of the modern Hybrid Teas and their influence shows through in these to considerable extent, the main differences being in their habit of growth, Hybrid Perpetuals being generally taller and more straggly.

Throughout the reign of Queen Victoria, when large, highly scented flowers were much valued, they enjoyed great popularity. Few large gardens were without at least some Hybrid Perpetuals.

There are some interesting and unusual members of this family. 'Baron Girod de l'Ain' (page 85) and 'Roger Lambelin' both have their petals delicately edged with white. 'Ferdinand Pichard' (page 47) introduced slightly later, is one of the boldest striped roses available even today and 'Mrs John Laing' (page 44) is an asset to any modern garden. Two others I would hate to be without, of quieter colouring, are 'Paul's Early Blush' and 'Baroness Rothschild' (page 68), both have a very fine scent.

The growth habits of these old roses, although variable, permit their use in most situations – several are accommodating enough to live comfortably in the confines of a tub.

## Hybrid Teas

The credit for the first Hybrid Tea goes to Jean-Baptiste Guillot of France. In about 1860 he discovered a seedling different to others he had seen which he named 'La France' in 1867. It is believed to be the result of a cross between a Hybrid Perpetual and a Tea-scented rose. In shape of flower it was high centred and fully double. Its colour was soft pink. Its growth habit was tidy and it repeated regularly each season. It was the first of a race of roses that would eventually become the most popular of all and many hundreds of varieties have been raised and introduced since. Several of the early varieties are still with us today and are well worth garden space as first-class roses.

Henry Bennett was the first Britisher to work with Hybrid Teas and several of his roses were used as parents by other breeders of the day. Bennett in fact was the first breeder to hybridize to a planned programme and, although Guillot raised the first, the Englishman must go down as the real pioneer.

These days, Hybrid Teas, along with Floribundas, make up the bulk of the roses sold throughout the world. In form they usually have pointed buds and are full of well-arranged petals. Their uses range from bedding and group planting to exhibition and floristry. Most are scented to some degree or other. Over the last twenty years or so they have been heavily interbred with other types of roses, especially Floribundas, and, as a consequence, have been re-classified as Large Flowered Roses.

## Modern Shrub Roses

This is a slightly misleading name because many of these roses have been with us for many years and, while most of them do not qualify to be termed old-fashioned, several fit happily into that category. In fact, any rose from any era that does not immediately fit into a recognized group gets placed here, so Modern Shrub Roses are of varied and mixed ancestry.

Almost all have a long flowering season. Some of the most widely grown varieties are the purple 'Yesterday', the multicoloured 'Joseph's Coat', and the pink 'Fritz Nobis'. Their main asset is their versatility. Several excellent varieties can be used as climbers and pillar roses and others are ideal for hedging. Most of them are a little too bright and garish for my taste but, if the variety you seek is not available from the conventional groups then it is, invariably, to be found among the Modern Shrubs.

## Moschata Roses

*Rosa moschata* is believed to have been introduced some time during the reign of Henry VIII and since then it has played an important part in the evolution of modern roses, being involved initially in the creation of the Hybrid Musks and being a parent to the Noisettes and, through them, the Floribundas. Apart from these descendants, there are a few more directly related varieties, but these are of no real significance. Their most distinctive feature is their slenderish, drooping foliage, which is usually of greyish or lightish-green colouring. None bear large flowers but almost all have scent. They are late flowering – most of them start in July and go on well into autumn. For a time *R. moschata* was thought to have become extinct but in the 1960s Graham

Stuart Thomas rediscovered it and it has now become widely available once more.

## Moss Roses

Although they are generally referred to as Moss roses, most of the roses of this group are Centifolias. They probably originate from *Rosa centifolia* 'Muscosa', a sport from *R. centifolia*. One or two, however, are Damasks and others, especially recently, have been raised from complex crossings. During the 19th century, when most were raised, they appeared probably more by accident than intent, either as sports or chance seedlings from other Mosses. In some the moss is soft and whispy, in others no more than high density thorns like whiskers. Frequently the moss is aromatic, especially to touch.

The Moss roses have no particular niche or role to fill in the garden beyond that of a good flowering shrub. Most are not difficult to grow and some of the shorter varieties have a long flowering season. This makes them ideal subjects for pots and tubs.

## Multiflora Ramblers

There are few more pleasing sights in mid-summer than trusses of roses festooning an old tree and what better to choose for this purpose than a vigorous Multiflora Rambler – perhaps 'Bobbie James', 'Rambling Rector', or even *Rosa multiflora* itself.

Some of the more hybrid Multifloras, unlike the more vigorous kind, will often produce flowers well into autumn. 'Phyllis Bide', for example, one of the best, will flower until the frosts come in November. Most Multifloras have relatively few thorns so this gives them a further advantage, especially when children are active in the garden. Some of my favourites amongst this group of ramblers are the blues and purples – 'Violette', 'Veilchenblau', and 'Bleu Magenta', which, although only summer flowering, combine so well with the softer creams and whites.

*R. multiflora* has not made its mark only in the garden. It has also played a major part in the development of other groups. Amongst its long list of descendants are the Hybrid Musks, the Dwarf Polyanthas, the modern-day Floribundas, and several of the newer Procumbents.

## Noisette Roses

John Champney of America introduced the first Noisette rose, believed to be a cross between the China Rose 'Parson's Pink' (now known as 'Old Blush') and *Rosa moschata*. Champney sent the resulting seedlings to his friend Philippe Noisette, who sent them on to his brother Louis, who was a nurseryman in Paris. Louis soon realized their potential and introduced the first one under the name of 'Rosier de Philippe Noisette'. After that they never looked back, because for the first time continuous-flowering roses were available to an eager public. Several of the early Noisettes are still with us today, including the beautiful 'Champney's Pink Cluster', which is thought to be one of Champney's original seedlings. Raisers continued to introduce Noisettes well into the 19th century and one of the best-selling climbing roses even today is the beautiful Noisette 'Mme Alfred Carrière', raised in 1879.

## Pimpinellifolia Roses

*Rosa pimpinellifolia*, until recently known as *R. spinosissima*, is native to Europe. It grew in areas where soil and climate were not always the most congenial, which is why roses of its group are so easy to grow in almost any soil. The garden forms known as the Scotch or Burnet roses were first popularized by the Brown brothers of Perth, Scotland, in 1793. One of the brothers found a wild double form that he raised and then, by continually sowing the seeds, from this seedling raised many more, and so on, eventually producing dozens of varieties.

All the Burnets have fern-like foliage consisting of many tiny, dark, serrated leaflets and most, especially the single varieties, follow their flowers with a display of mahogany or dark brown, shiny, rounded hips. All are viciously armed with numerous sharp spines. In the garden they will tolerate even the poorest soil and are not too unhappy in semi-shade. They never outgrow their welcome and, except for a few hybrids, seldom get taller than 4ft (1.2m). The flowers are produced in great profusion for about three weeks in late June. In the first half of the last century these roses were used extensively to create short, dense hedges. It would be pleasant to see more planted for this purpose today.

## Portland Roses

There has to be some doubt about the true origin of the Portland roses. The first, 'Duchess of Portland' (page 98), is said to have been the result of a cross between 'Slater's Crimson China' and a seedling that was itself a cross between *Rosa damascena bifera* and an unknown Gallica. However, any controversy as to the origins or parentage cannot overshadow the importance of the rose, for, after it arrived in France in the late 18th century it yielded several interesting offspring, which became known as the Portland Damasks. The first Portland variety bred from the 'Duchess of Portland' was 'Rose du Roi', a purple, short-growing, fairly double, remontant variety.

Several good Portlands are still listed by the specialists in old roses, the best known being 'Comte de Chambord' of 1860. They are all remontant and the advantage they have over many of the old varieties is their tidy, short, stocky habit of growth. This lends them to many uses in the smaller garden, from hedging to group planting. They are particularly useful as container plants for the terrace or patio, especially as all are well endowed with fragrance. Their only real fault is a dislike of wet weather while in flower, but this is because of the high density of the petals.

## Procumbent Roses

In recent years the demand for low-growing, spreading roses has increased and breeders have fulfilled this need with considerable success. These roses are used for massed display and as economical ground-cover, as well as for hiding manhole covers, trailing over walls and pots, and even cascading from large hanging baskets. They are also effective at the edge of the water and many can tolerate the shade of other taller varieties in the shrubbery.

'Nozomi' and 'The Fairy' (page 68) are both excellent and popular varieties, but the range gets bigger every year. One recent variety that I particularly like is 'Pink Bells', with its compact growing habit and masses of pompon-like flowers.

Wide-growing roses are by no means new, it is just that they have come into vogue. The Victorians and Edwardians used Ramblers for covering banks and awkward open spaces with considerable success and,

for those who seek size today, *Rosa wichuraiana* is well worth trying.

## Rugosa Roses

For toughness and resilience the Rugosa roses are hard to beat, but sadly, for this reason, they are too often thought of as hedging plants with little more to offer. While undoubtedly they do make excellent hedges, most varieties also make superb specimen and border subjects. All of them will give a good display of flowers throughout the season and many offer the added luxury of autumn colour and large, vivid, globular hips. The style of their flowers is diverse, from the large, single, crêpe-textured flowers of 'Scabrosa' (page 78) and *Rosa rugosa* 'Alba' (page 34) to the large, blowsy, full blooms of 'Vanguard', not to mention the Grootendorst range, which have fimbriated, dianthus-like clusters.

The origins of these roses lie in Japan. They were brought to Europe towards the end of the 19th century and many hybrids have been introduced since then. Those with their ancestry nearer to the original species are rudely healthy but some of the late hybrids have a tendency to suffer from rust. In most cases though this occurs late in the season so it should not be allowed to detract too much from their high value as garden plants.

## Sweetbriers or Eglanteria Roses

Most of the Sweetbriers have scented flowers but it is their aromatic foliage that gives them their name. It is a pleasant smell and it is at its best when the foliage is young and tender. In days gone by, these roses, especially the wild species *Rosa eglanteria*, were used in the preparation of potions and medicines and they were also used in the making of mead.

Towards the end of the 1800s, an Englishman, Lord Penzance, bred and introduced more than fifteen varieties, among them a variety called 'Lady Penzance' which is probably the best known today and, without doubt, the most strongly scented. One Sweetbrier too frequently overlooked when planning shrubberies is 'Manning's Blush' (page 56), a fully double white dating back to 1830. It is less vigorous than most and repeats its flowers occasionally. The majority of Sweetbriers, however, flower only once each season and most have single flowers that provide the added bonus of hips in the autumn. The few with double flowers tend to have larger leaves, which are aromatic, only when crushed.

Although, for some tastes, their growth habits are a little coarse, these roses can be put to a variety of uses; they make big shrubs and fit perfectly into the wild garden or natural setting. They also make excellent hedges, especially in rural areas where they are congenial to the countryside. I have also seen them used to good effect as climbers.

### Tea-scented Roses

The first Tea-scented rose to find its way to Europe was *Rosa indica odorata* later known as 'Hume's Blush' after Sir Abraham Hume, who was responsible for sending it from Canton in China in 1810. The second was found, soon after, by a plant-collecting expedition sent to China by Britain's Royal Horticultural Society. It was named 'Parks' Yellow Tea-scented China', the name by which it is still known today. All Tea Roses originate from the species *R. gigantea*. Many of the other early Tea Roses were transported to Europe aboard ships belonging to the East India Tea Company and this reflects in their name. They soon became very popular, especially in warmer areas of Europe, such as the south of France. The Victorians were very partial to them and grew the less hardy varieties in cold greenhouses or conservatories, using them for buttonholes and cut flowers.

Tea Roses often have slightly sprawly habits of growth and are sometimes rather lacking in foliage for modern tastes, but these traits should deter no one from growing them, for among their ranks are some of the most beautiful of roses.

### Wichuraiana Roses

This family of roses includes many old favourites of almost every garden before the war. Members of my grandparents' generation seldom fail to mention 'Albertine' (page 84), 'Dorothy Perkins', and 'Albéric Barbier' (page 106) when talking of their childhood gardens.

It is to the credit of these varieties that they are still almost as popular today, and so they should be, for they are excellent roses. Most have good, healthy, glossy foliage only occasionally marred by mildew and several will produce the odd second flush in autumn. The best of the bunch though is surely 'New Dawn', a sport from 'Dr W. van Fleet'. It flowers continually from June to October and will tolerate even the leanest soil.

# 2

# OLD-FASHIONED ROSES IN THE GARDEN

Nearly every garden has a gap, unfilled because it is thought that nothing will survive there. Numerous situations come to mind – north-facing walls, patches of poor soil, shaded areas. So, why not try a rose? They are relatively inexpensive as plants go and they are tolerant of most things. In the end it may prove impossible but, if you enjoy roses, very little has been lost.

## North-facing Situations

There are many bare, north-facing walls that would look much more attractive if adorned by a rose and many north-facing borders that would benefit from the addition of a few old garden roses. They may never do as well as their catalogue specifications but, if you sympathize with their problems, they will usually respond. Quite a few Climbers, Ramblers, and Shrub roses are available and one of the reasons that careful choice is important is that they will always be a little more at risk from the perils of weather than roses in warmer situations. Therefore, during their first season, protect them with some form of windbreak, perhaps one constructed of polythene and bamboo canes.

It is important to any rose to have a good start in life but, when it is expected to cope with the additional problems of shade and cold, it is vital. Dig some manure into the ground before planting and make sure the plant is secured to the wall or support to prevent windrock. Once it is growing, top dress with rose fertilizer regularly, but especially in late spring. Do not feed them after flowering, especially with nitrogen as this will encourage young, soft

growth and render the plant more susceptible to the ravages of winter. Any frost damage that does occur should be trimmed away at pruning time to prevent further dieback and keep the plant in trim.

Although there are some that repeat, the majority of varieties that will tolerate north-facing situations flower only once each season, but some produce hips and others have good foliage. For recommendations, see pages 119–20 and 131–3.

## Shaded Areas

A dark area of the garden can prove difficult to fill, because not many summer-flowering plants will tolerate shade. Although most roses demand as much sunlight as possible there are some that will accept a certain amount of shade and a few that will tolerate quite a lot (for recommendations, see pages 120–1 and 133–4).

East- and west-facing aspects with shadows cast from behind usually get sun for at least half of the day and, in these and southerly situations, provided the soil is good, almost any rose is worth a try. It is northerly situations, with trees or buildings casting shadows from the south, that really present problems of choice.

## Poor Soils

Poor soil should not deter gardeners from growing old roses. Admittedly, the choice of varieties may be rather restricted, but there are enough varieties that will adapt to such conditions to make the effort worthwhile. In any case, such soil can usually be improved and, if the rules of good husbandry are observed, both in preparation of the ground and in after-care, roses will respond. For recommendations, see pages 121–3 and 134–5.

## Hedges

The varieties most commonly used for a rose hedge are those of the Rugosa family and, with the exception of just a few, they are an excellent choice. Most Rugosas have a long flowering season and several set large colourful hips. Several, too, develop autumn colouring and all are tough, robust, and impenetrable when mature. However, the Rugosas should not have it all their own way for there are numerous other types of roses suitable for this purpose. Even Ramblers, trained correctly, can make a strong and interesting hedge. A few fairly common varieties that have proved themselves as hedgerows are described on pages 123–5.

## Tree Climbers

Trees make ideal supports for the more vigorous Ramblers and Climbers; any tree can be used, dead or alive, short or tall. All will look lovely festooned with roses, especially after their own blossom is over. The selected varieties will need to be tolerant of shade and, to some extent, poorer soil. For suggestions, see page 136.

## The Smaller Garden

Sadly, gardens seem to be getting smaller. Lack of space however should not deter lovers of old roses from indulging themselves. There are many smaller varieties that will fit happily into small areas (see pages 125–6) and many ways of growing them to utilize space. A standard rose, for example, will take up only the minimum of space while still allowing room for other roses or plants to grow beneath it. Standards are also effective in the centre of a small bed, where they will add an extra dimension and will not mind the plants huddled below. If wall space is limited, climbers on pillars can be used to give the same effect. Many roses will live contentedly in the confines of a pot and, in some cases, even a hanging basket, and there are many shorter-growing old roses that are quite happy growing cheek by jowl with other plants in the herbaceous or mixed borders of the garden.

## Tubs and Pots

Many plants can be grown in pots and tubs. Favourites seem to be geraniums and fuchsias. These are both half-hardy and need to be treated with extra care in winter. As for more shrubby plants, conifers and heathers are the most common, seldom roses, except perhaps miniatures and modern patio roses. Roses of all types, however, actually quite enjoy growing in pots. For years now our display at the Chelsea Flower Show has been made up of roses grown entirely in this way and many varieties are now several years old. The shorter-growing varieties are, of course, best but, by careful choice of variety and attention to their special needs, even the vigorous ones will flourish (for suggestions, see pages 127–8). Even Climbers and Ramblers can be grown successfully in this way – the more sprawly of these look splendid untrained, tumbling over the sides of tubs or on a small trellis or a wall. In addition to conventional terracotta or concrete pots and urns, a large range of different types of containers can be utilized, from hollowed-out tree stumps to half barrels or purpose-built wooden boxes. Raised brick or stone structures also look good, especially as part of a terrace or patio.

Whatever the choice of container it is vital that it has sufficient drainage, otherwise the compost will become waterlogged and the plant unhappy. Do this by placing about 1–2in (2–5cm) of shingle in the bottom before potting. Another golden rule is never to allow the soil to become dry. The best compost to use for roses grown in containers is a mixture of seven parts loam, three parts peat, and one part sharp sand with added fertilizer.

Throughout its life the rose in a container will require regular feeding. Proprietary brands of rose fertilizer will provide the correct nutrients and are easily applied by simply sprinkling a handful on the surface of the soil and watering in. This should be done at least three times a year, once before growth starts in the spring, once just before flowering, followed by another at about the end of July. Add a little lime to the first feed.

Every three or four years a change of compost will be necessary. This should be done during the dormant season when the growth of the plant will not be disturbed.

## Greenhouses and Conservatories

Unless you are lucky enough to live in a very warm, sunny climate, there are several wonderful older roses whose full splendour cannot be fully appreciated until they are seen in the controlled environment of a greenhouse or conservatory. For recommendations, see pages 128-9 and 137.

Some of the more tender Climbers and Ramblers, especially Teas and Noisettes, also look magnificent when grown under glass.

## A Scented Garden

Scent is an asset to any garden and old roses, chosen with care, can play an important role in providing this. Various types of fragrance can be found among their ranks. All members of the Sweetbrier family, for example, emit a perfume reminiscent of apples, from both flowers and foliage. The Rugosas too, or at least some of them, also have a fruity smell and Tea Roses are said to have got their name because of their scent. The scent of the Albas, although pervading, is light and delicate, while that of the Mosses, Centifolias, and Gallicas is dense and heady. Of all the different fragrances, that of the Damask rose is probably the purest, which is why Damasks have been used in the manufacture of perfume throughout the centuries. For recommendations for roses to add scent to the garden, see pages 129-30 and 138.

## Roses as Companion Plants

Borders and beds entirely devoted to roses look very effective, but old roses make congenial companions for a wide variety of other plants. I like to grow my roses among as wide a variety of other subjects as possible – in the kitchen garden, for example, among the vegetables and herbs. Herbaceous and mixed borders with roses scattered here and there can be a delight. Rose beds are enhanced by a suitable edging and a number of shrubs and herbaceous plants are ideal for this purpose, amongst them box (*Buxus sempervirens*), lavender (in particular *Lavandula angustifolia* 'Munstead') and the superb, plum-coloured, dwarf *Berberis thunbergii* 'Atropurpurea'.

When beds are devoted entirely to old roses, I like to use ground cover where possible, and one of my favourites for this is the saxifrage 'London Pride', which spreads quickly and never gets too tall. Old roses always look good combined with grey-foliage plants, such as lamb's ears (*Stachys lanata*) and *Ballota pseudodictamnus*, and I love to see them with delphiniums, scabious, and geraniums, especially where climbing roses are forming a background. Clematis and honeysuckle are excellent companions for climbing roses and some interesting colour schemes can be created when these are mixed and matched.

## The Wild Garden

Many older roses, because of their growth habits, fit easily into natural and wild gardens, but the best are those with single flowers, especially those that give a good crop of hips. One obvious choice is *Rosa canina*, the common dog rose, and some of its hybrids, such as 'Andersonii' and 'Abbotswood'. Another is *R. arvensis*, the field rose, which is very vigorous and quite at home in shade, creeping among and through other shrubs. *R. pimpinellifolia* and many of its hybrids adapt readily to naturalization, even in the poorest soils. All three of these look wonderful in the wild garden, growing happily amidst the likes of snowdrops, blackberries, and foxgloves.

## Coastal Regions

While roses do not enjoy growing exposed to the sea, most will do well in coastal regions. Often, in fact, it is possible to grow some of the more tender varieties more successfully there than further inland because in the coastal regions winter frosts tend to be less severe. The biggest adverse condition will be wind from the sea so, if some form of windbreak is provided or a sheltered spot found, it is possible to be quite adventurous in choice of varieties.

## Flower Arrangements

Whether you are a keen flower arranger or just someone who likes to have the odd rose bloom around the house, it is surely more satisfying to use roses from your own garden than to purchase them – especially as few old roses are generally available from flower shops and those that are tend to be rather forced and immaculate. Nearly any rose can be cut without detriment to the plant. Although many tend to have a short vase life, some will last for several days, provided the temperature in the house is not too high. Some roses also have interesting foliage and this, too, can be a valuable asset to a flower arranger – *Rosa rubrifolia*, for example, has purplish-blue leaves that turn to red in the autumn. Hips, too, are useful for autumn arrangements and these come in many shapes and shades.

When cutting roses, never cut them with longer stems than necessary for the vase you have in mind and always give them a drink for several hours before arranging them. Crushing the end of their stems to help them take up water is also important and I always add a little sugar to the water in the vase as this helps them to stay fresh for a day or two longer.

# 3

# CULTIVATION

**Soils**

If allowed to choose their own soil, the older roses would select a clay-based loam with a pH of between 6 and 6.5, but they are not so fussy that they will not grow in other less desirable soils, both acid and alkaline. A soil with a pH around this level is neutral to slightly acid. It is very easy to test for acidity with a test kit, which can be purchased from any garden centre or shop. Although roses prefer slight acidity, alkaline soils will not upset the majority unduly.

Soils can always be improved, but doing so takes time and can be laborious. More often it is enough to accept the soil as it is, incorporating organic material and fertilizer when planting. The plant will soon become established enough to fend for itself, and will merely need feeding each spring thereafter. If soil is particularly poor more drastic action may be necessary, but most old roses are quite willing to adapt themselves to most given situations.

Good drainage is important too, for few roses will tolerate waterlogged ground. Poorly drained soil does not allow sufficient oxygen to their roots and will take longer to warm up in the spring than freely drained soil. The addition of sand or gravel to the soil when planting may help but, if the soil is really waterlogged, proper land drains should be introduced. Alternatively, if the soil is too well drained, plenty of peat or organic matter will help counteract this, by conserving moisture in very dry weather or drought. Alkaline soils usually have a high proportion of lime and chalk present, so the addition of peat or farmyard manure will help reduce alkalinity as well as improve their water-holding capabilities. If

soil is found to be too acid, it will benefit from regular applications of calcium in the form of lime.

**Preparation of the Ground**

Whatever the type of soil, it is always advisable to prepare the ground well before planting. The hard work necessary for this will be repaid handsomely by healthier, stronger plants in later years. If completely new beds or borders are being created, and you are not averse to the use of chemicals, then the area should first be sprayed during the growing season with a good, complete weedkiller. This will rid the soil of most perennial weeds, but not the recently cast seed. To banish seedlings and annual weeds it is best to allow them to germinate and then spray with a contact weedkiller two or three times during the summer prior to planting – remember, one year's seeds are seven years' weeds. Alternatively, if chemical weed-control offends, then perennial weeds should be removed with a fork, taking care not to leave any pieces of root behind, or new weeds will quickly grow. Annual weeds are best dug-in before they seed themselves, for they will help provide extra organic material to the soil. If time permits, ground should be dug over before winter and left untouched, it will then benefit, as it breaks down, from the action of frost.

**Specific Replant Disease**

Roses do not enjoy growing in the soil from which other roses have been removed. If the soil cannot be changed then it must be given a rest from roses for at least twelve months before any new roses can be grown in it. It is for this reason that professional rose growers rotate their crops on different pieces of land from year to year. Roses suffering from specific replant disease (sometimes called rose sickness) will appear stunted and never give of their best. The disease is caused by certain chemicals secreted into the soil by the old plants. Always resist the temptation to ignore this rule or treat it as an old wives' tale. There is little point in paying good money for roses if they are not going to do well.

## Feeding Roses

It is important to give roses a good start in life by feeding them well at planting time. Well-rotted farmyard manure is probably best, but if this is not readily available a mixture of one handful of bonemeal to a bucket of peat makes a good substitute. Each rose should receive a heaped double-handful. Broadcasting bonemeal at about 1oz/sq. yd (4g/sq. m), or an equivalent amount of a slow-release fertilizer, just prior to planting, especially if the soil is poor, will also do good. The advantage of slow-release fertilizer is that its nutrients are released gradually through a period of several months. These fertilizers can also be used as top dressing on established roses. This is best done just before the growth starts in spring, perhaps at the same time as pruning, when April showers will help it permeate into the soil, to reach the roots just as they start to become active. One early top dressing should be enough, but, on poorer soils, an extra feed in early summer will help the plant recover from its first flush of flowers and sustain it into winter. Make sure that fertilizers are well balanced; too much nitrogen will cause excessive growth and not enough potash will result in fewer flowers, of poorer quality. Roses need plenty of potash, so it is difficult to overfeed with this. Trace elements are also important, so make sure that the fertilizer contains a balance of these. Pot-grown roses will need fertilizer regularly throughout their life, because nutrients are leached from potting mediums more quickly than from garden soils. Liquid fertilizers are available and easy to use and I find pot-grown roses respond well to this treatment. Roses will also respond to foliar feeding, but this must be done in the evening to avoid the danger of strong sunshine scorching the leaves.

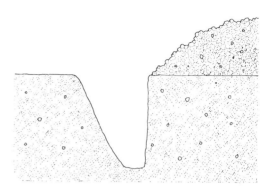

If you are heeling in a rose, dig a trench and pile the soil on the straight side.

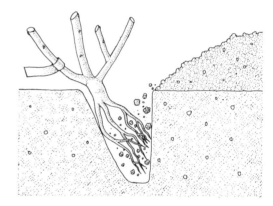

Place the rose against the slanting side, and push soil into the trench.

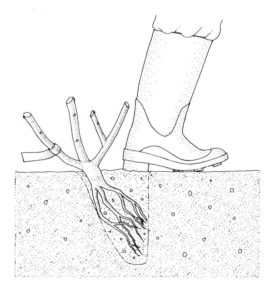

Use the heel of your boot to make sure that the soil around the rose is firm.

## Planting Bare-root Roses

The majority of bare-root roses are purchased in late autumn, winter, or early spring straight from the nursery. On arrival, if they cannot be planted immediately, they should be temporarily heeled-in to prevent them from drying out. If the weather is frosty, an area of ground should be covered, in anticipation of their arrival, by a piece of sacking or some such material. This will provide a frost-free holding area until the weather improves for planting. To heel them in, dig a trench deep enough to accommodate all the roots. A slightly slanted trench is best, so that the roses can be placed at an angle of about 45°, and well covered with soil to above root level. This angle also ensures that the plants can be trodden in firmly to keep out any future frost. It is much better to select a sheltered position for heeling-in roses if possible.

When planting, dig the hole deep and wide enough to cover the union and avoid any cramping of the roots. The soil in the bottom of the hole should be loosened and a couple of handfuls of mixed peat and bonemeal added and mixed in well with the spade. It is also a good plan to throw a further handful of the same mixture on to the pile of soil to be returned into the hole with the plant. Again, when planting, it is important to wear good leather gloves so that you can hold the rose firmly by the stem as it is placed into the hole. Ensure that the roots are well spread, then put back about half the soil, shaking the rose slightly so that there are no soil-free pockets left among the roots. At this halfway stage, tread in lightly with the foot and then add most of the remainder of the soil, once again treading it firmly. Firm planting helps prevent windrock and will deter suckers later in the life of the plant. When satisfied that the plant is secure in the soil, at the correct depth, return the remaining soil. Labelling should be done at this time, if not before – it is surprising how quickly names can be forgotten!

The shoots of autumn-planted roses should be pruned to about half their length to help prevent windrock during winter. Those planted in spring should be pruned back much harder, firstly to help avoid too much dehydration from drying out and, secondly, to encourage any new growth to come from the base of the plant.

When you plant a bare-root rose, dig a hole large enough to accommodate the roots. Add a little peat and bone meal if required, mixing it into the soil at the base of the hole or into the soil you have taken out of the hole.

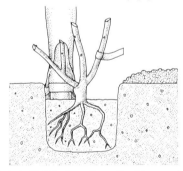

Place the rose in the hole, making sure that the roots are well spread and that the rose is at the correct depth. Begin to push the soil back into the hole, shaking the plant a little to ensure that the soil covers the roots and fills any gaps.

When the hole is half full, firm the soil with your heel.

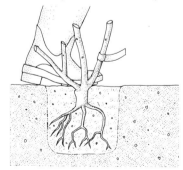

When all the soil has been replaced in the hole, firm the surface carefully.

## Planting Container-grown Roses

From late spring through the summer to early autumn any roses purchased will almost certainly be containerized, usually in a polythene-bag pot. In many ways container-grown roses are easier to plant than bare-root plants.

It is important not to disturb any of the compost around the roots, so, after digging the hole, first remove the bottom of the polythene container with a sharp knife, then place the rose into the hole with the remainder of the pot still intact. Once in position, having ensured the correct depth to cover the union, slit the side of the pot and peel it away. Infill around the roots and firm carefully, tidying the soil surface at the end of the operation.

The compost used in growing container roses is usually made up largely of peat and, if this is allowed to dry out, it is very difficult to remoisten, so make sure that the ball of soil is well soaked before planting. Also ensure that newly or recently planted container-grown roses are watered regularly for several weeks, at least until you are satisfied that the root system has expanded enough to be getting moisture from the surrounding new soil.

## Planting Climbing and Rambling Roses

The method employed in planting climbers or ramblers is much the same as that for shrub or bush roses. However, the position or site in which it is to grow will have a bearing on the way it is done. If the rose is to grow on a wall of a house then the hole should be dug at least 6in (15cm) away from the foundations, because the soil next to houses is often poorer than elsewhere in the garden and is also drier, especially when the aspect is southerly. It is therefore wise to add extra peat and bonemeal at planting time. Vigorous roses will have to be watered at regular intervals at least during the first year of growth – they have much more foliage than shorter types and they lose water far more rapidly.

If roses are to be trained against a trellis or on pillars or fences, then the structure should be positioned first, otherwise the rose will be disturbed while the support is under construction.

It is sometimes thought that plants on the walls of houses cause unnecessary dampness and that their roots will disturb the foundations. I very much doubt this. Roots invariably move away from the walls in search of wetter, more nourishing soil, and most roses shed their leaves in winter when the danger of encouraging dampness is at its worst.

## Planting Standard Roses

When planting a standard rose a good strong stake should be driven in first. Square, wooden stakes are best, though round, rustic poles can also look effective. In either case, their useful life is prolonged if they are treated with some sort of wood preservative. Most stakes will need replacing at least once during the lifetime of a rose, so it is well worth planning for this eventuality by inserting a drainpipe

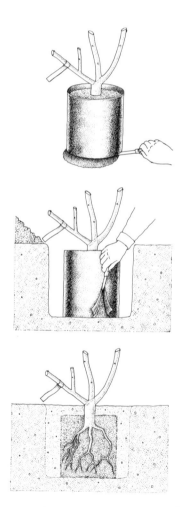

When planting a container-grown rose, remove the base of the container before the rest of pot and placing the rose in the already-prepared hole.

into the ground first. This will enable any replacement stake to be put in position with the minimum of disturbance. After the stake is positioned, planting is carried out in much the same way as with shrubs or bushes. With a standard, though, there is no union from which the depth of planting can be gauged, so a good guide is to cover the uppermost roots with about 2in (5cm) of soil. Ideally, the stem should be about $1\frac{1}{2}$in (4cm) from the stake. The height of the stake is also important. I prefer to see the top about 1in (2.5cm) below the crown of the plant. The stem should be secured to the stake in at least two places by good strong straps. Umbrella-shaped wire frames are available for training weeping standards to weep. These are not essential but can be helpful where formality is important. However, I prefer to see them less formally trained or allowed to grow to the ground naturally. The golden rules for all newly planted standards is to keep them well watered, all through their first season. They will take a long time to recover if they are ever allowed to become too dry.

## Pruning

As opposed to the hard pruning applied to modern Hybrid Teas and Floribundas, most old garden roses need only be tidied from time to time. In the first year only is hard pruning important to encourage growth from the base. Often, once the shrub is established, it will only be necessary to shorten the odd, straggly branch or cut out old or diseased wood. There are no hard and fast rules, though one or two rules of thumb are applicable to the different groups. However, if a year goes by without any pruning, no old rose will suffer unduly.

Bearing in mind the rules of thumb, I will deal with the various groups separately, but remember that with all roses it is important to remove all diseased wood – the smallest piece overlooked may cause problems another year. Also, try to prune to prevent stems rubbing against each other – chafing leaves the way open for disease to enter, especially stem canker.

### Climbers and Ramblers

Before deciding how to tackle Climbers and Ramblers, it is necessary to know whether they flower on

wood made in the same season or on growth produced the previous year. The group that flowers on wood made in the same season are the Climbers, among them the Noisettes, climbing Teas, Hybrid Teas, and Hybrid Perpetuals. Climbers are growing and producing flowers at the same time, so pruning is as much related to training shoots and encouraging them to grow in various ways as it is to cutting out wood. Long, vigorous shoots should be tied in as many different directions as possible, bearing in mind that the way they are trained will affect the overall appearance of the plant as it gets older and that these shoots will become in due course the main stems that will produce lateral stems. Each year all the laterals can be cut back to as much as two-thirds of their length; it is from these that most of the flowers will be produced. In this way, by leaving a strong lateral here and there untouched to become a main shoot in its turn, a pattern is evolved that will

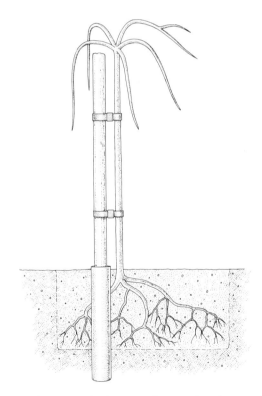

When you plant a standard rose, make sure that the top of the stake is 1in (2.5cm) below the level of the crown. Place the stake on the side of the prevailing wind and use at least two ties.

encourage regular flowering as well as adequate growth.

It is the Ramblers that produce flowers on growth made in the previous season. Wichuraiana and Multiflora hybrids belong in this group, as do the hybrids of *Rosa arvensis* and *R. sempervirens* and some of the species, such as *R. filipes*. It is best to leave these roses for the first two or three years to allow them to get a good start. When pruning is undertaken it is best done in the summer, immediately after flowering. This allows the plant to make more growth on which to produce its flowers the following year. Because they produce their flowers on older wood, the more shoots that are left the better they will flower, so confine any surgery to the removal of those old branches that are no longer producing enough growth to support flowers. The more vigorous tree-climbing ramblers are better left entirely to their own devices.

*Weeping Standards*

Weeping standards are actually varieties of Ramblers budded on to stems. Therefore the growth they make in one season will determine the flower production the next. For these, hard pruning by the removal of older, spent wood in the dormant season can be combined with a light trimming after flowering. Sometimes awkward shoots refuse to weep and grow upwards, these should be cut away completely or shortened; especially if they appear from the top of the plant. Even when stems have been trained downwards, their lateral growths will sometimes grow upwards in search of the sun; these should be tied in or cut back slightly after the flowers are over.

There are several ways of training weeping standards. The easiest and least unsightly is to tie the long, flexible stems to the stake that is supporting them, using unobtrusive green string or wire. Alternatively, an umbrella-like frame can be purchased. This is placed at the top of the standard and fixed to the supporting stake with the branches tucked beneath it. This means of training is probably the most effective but it can look somewhat contrived. The third method is to place a wire hoop, attached to stakes, around the standard at about 3ft (1m) from the ground. Shoots can then be pulled down to the wire and secured to it. This method is best for the

very vigorous varieties. Finally, the easiest method of all is to tie string or wire loosely around all the shoots in order to keep them drooping to the ground.

*Shrubs and Older Roses*

These are easier to prune than Climbers and Ramblers but, again, they fall into several different groups. Hybrid Musks, Hybrid Perpetuals, and Portlands do not mind being hard pruned and, in fact, will benefit considerably from such treatment. The Bourbon roses, too, are reasonably tolerant of regular trimming. However, it is perhaps better to be somewhat more gentle with these, only removing spindly and wayward shoots, cutting back other stems only moderately to keep them in shape, and removing wood that is causing the plant to become overcrowded, especially in the centre. All these types should be pruned in late winter to early spring, when the possibility of really heavy frosts is diminishing.

As regards the much older groups such as the Damasks, Centifolias, and Gallicas these will not require very much attention. Most pruning should be done after flowering, which gives the plants the chance to replenish their flowering wood for the following year. Leggy growths should be cut back and perhaps, if the plants have become very dense, tough wood should be removed or reduced to about one-third of its length. If plants have been badly neglected and more severe treatment is thought necessary then this should be done in the dormant season. Such treatment will benefit the plants in the long run but will probably impede flowering in the following year. Part of the charm and character of many of the old roses is in their growth habits and care should be taken not to destroy this by over-pruning at any stage of their life after the first year. This is why I favour close-density planting and little pruning. They can then entwine with each other and together give the most stunning display. In some cases where they are particularly vigorous and sprawly it may be necessary to use man-made structures to support them. A simple square frame for the rose to lean on, about 18in (45cm) from the ground, with stakes at each corner, is the easiest way. Structures made of unobtrusive rustic logs can also be used and, in the case of the very vigorous varieties, a tripod of rustic stakes, around which the rose can become entangled, can be most effective.

### Rose Hedges and Procumbents

Roses used as hedges have to be treated quite differently to those grown as shrubs, for, if they are left unpruned, a very sparse hedge may result. This does depend somewhat on the varieties, but by following the general rules of thumb already mentioned, it should not be too difficult to prune any hedge. In all cases, newly planted rose hedges must be hard pruned.

The most common rose hedge is that of the Rugosa varieties. These are usually fairly dense by nature, so, once they are established, a once-a-year trim in winter should keep them in shape.

Procumbent roses do not require too much attention – the object with these is to keep them as dense as possible – and, as far as pruning goes, it is just a case of removing dead or spent wood when necessary and removing upward growing shoots. If the more vigorous varieties get out of hand, they can be cut back hard if desired without coming to any real long-term harm.

## Rejuvenating Old Roses

Sometimes an old rose that has suffered neglect is inherited when you move house. This may be very difficult to revive, and it is often better to dig it out and start again with another. However, if you wish to rejuvenate it, do so by moderate pruning, perhaps reducing any shoots to a third of their length and removing some of the very old wood – but beware, over-enthusiastic pruning of a rose that may be many years old may prove too much for it. If however, an old rose that has seen better days is an old friend or particularly beautiful, then it may be worth having a new plant specially grown from it. Many professional rose growers offer a propagation service and will produce new plants from old material. Many old and rare varieties have been saved from extinction in this way.

## Dead-heading

The removal of unsightly dead or spent flowers from rose bushes, especially old fashioneds, is important not only to the eye but to the well being of the plant.

They should be neatly snipped off at the first leaf bud below the cluster. Doing it this way vastly improves the overall appearance of the plant and encourages new growth to sprout more quickly. In the case of the repeat-flowering shrub roses, dead-heading induces far more flowers in the second flush and, in the case of the summer flowering shrubs such as the Damasks, Gallicas, and Centifolias, this light summer pruning will result in more flowering shoots for next season. It must be remembered, though, that lots of species and several varieties of shrub roses produce excellent, decorative hips in the autumn so do not dead head these, no matter how unsightly the flowers may look in decay.

## Suckers

The part of the rose bush that grows above the ground – i.e., the shoots – has been induced, by the nurseryman who produced it, to adopt its roots from another rose. The reason for this is that the process of propagation, known as budding, is the most efficient means of producing roses commercially. The process of budding is explained in more detail elsewhere in the book but, in order to explain suckers it is worth mentioning here that a nodal bud from a named variety is placed into a rootstock of a wild rose. When this bud starts to grow, the visible parts of the rootstock are cut away, leaving the bud

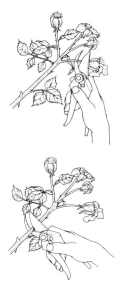

*Top*: the incorrect way to dead head a rose, and, *above*, the correct way to remove dead flower heads.

to grow from the roots. As the new plant grows, it is natural that, from time to time, the roots fight back and try to dominate by sending up shoots of their own. It is these that are called suckers. Because the rootstock is usually more vigorous than its adopted variety the suckers will eventually take over and must, therefore, be removed.

Recognizing a sucker is sometimes difficult and, to be sure, it is wise to trace it back to its source. On every rose bush there is a slight bulge between root and stem called the union – this is where the original bud was placed. If the doubtful shoot is growing from below this bulge, it is most certainly a sucker. The best method of removal is by pulling it away from the roots but, unless the sucker is quite young, this may be found to be too difficult, so a blunt instrument of some sort such as a broken-off kitchen knife may help. Cutting away the sucker with a sharp knife is not a good idea as this method often leaves a short stump from which even more suckers will grow. Unwelcome shoots, in the form of suckers, will also be found, now and then, growing from the stems of standards, especially when they are young. These are easily picked or pushed off with the thumb and finger if caught early enough.

Much can be done to reduce the incidence of suckers if care is taken to observe some simple rules. When planting, bear in mind that suckers often appear from wounds, so take care not to damage any roots with the spade. Deep planting is also important. If any part of the rootstock is above ground it will grow on its own accord.

## Prince Charles

This rose has large, muddled flowers of crimson-purple that are abundant only in mid-summer. Heavily veined, they fade slightly to dull maroon, but are enhanced by white tinges at the base of their petals and bright yellow anthers. Broad leaves of bright green cloak this somewhat sprawly shrub, which can be contained if supported but is best allowed to arch gracefully if space will permit. It makes an excellent companion to roses of paler shades because, if used cleverly, it helps to accentuate their quieter colours. If 'Souvenir de la Malmaison', for example, is planted nearby, it will look even more delicate while accentuating the deeper colour and darker foliage of 'Prince Charles'. Despite its short flowering season, this is an excellent rose that will tolerate shade and grow in inferior soil.
Bourbon
Date unknown
Summer flowering
5 × 4ft (1.5 × 1.2m)

## Rosa rugosa Alba

Rugosa roses are extremely popular for many reasons, and the pure white, highly scented *Rosa rugosa* 'Alba' is excellent. Its flowers are composed of five large petals and brilliant yellow stamens, and although they fall earlier than those of the more double varieties, are followed by large, vermilion hips, rich in Vitamin C. The tough, dark green leaves are heavily veined. In the autumn, while the plant is still adorned with hips, they take on stunning shades of yellow and gold before falling to expose thorny, greyish stems. *Rosa rugosa* 'Alba' makes an excellent hedge and can be mixed with other Rugosas to good effect.
Rugosa
*c.*1870
Repeat flowering
7 × 6ft (2.1 × 1.8m)

**Eugénie Guinoisseau**
When the cupped flower is
young, its velvety petals are a
vivid shade of magenta-purple
but, sadly, as they age they fade
to lilac-grey and dull mauve.
They are scrolled and furled,
often hiding a central green eye.
Foliage is slightly glossy,
darkish green, smooth and
circular, concealing to some
extent a very deep green moss.
The plant will benefit from
support of some kind and is
perhaps best closely planted
with other roses, when its
slightly sprawling habit can be
disguised. A repeat flowering
sometimes occurs, but this
cannot be relied upon. It is
tolerant of poorer soil.
Centifolia Moss
1864
Summer flowering (occasional
repeats)
6 × 4ft (1.8 × 1.2m)

**Belle Poitevine**
Flat, slightly irregularly formed
flowers emerge from thin,
pointed buds. The muddled
mid-pink petals surround pale,
creamy yellow stamens. The
flowers are followed by large,
dark red hips that do not always
fully develop. Coarse, heavily
veined, dark green foliage takes
on a lovely autumn colouring of
golden yellow. The plant is
thickset and prickly. It is useful
as a border shrub and for
hedging, as well as making an
effective specimen shrub.
Rugosa
1894
Repeat flowering
6 × 5ft (1.8 × 1.5m)

**Louise Odier**
This rose draws attention because of its scent and glamorous, rose-pink flowers. These are near perfect in shape, with the outer petals forming a globe around numerous inner ones. Borne in clusters, the flowers are present on the bush for most of the summer months. The leaves are refreshingly green and, like the flowers, almost perfect in shape. Vigorous in growth, the branches sometimes bend gracefully with the weight of the flowers. To add to the merits of this rose, it is tolerant of shade and, although it prefers good soil, will not mind if asked to grow in poor conditions.
Bourbon
1851
Continuous flowering
5 × 4ft (1.5 × 1.2m)

## Papa Hémeray

For a China rose this has fairly dense growth and very few thorns; in many ways it is more typical of a Dwarf Polyantha, for most Chinas tend to be more spindly and have fewer leaves. The small, single, bright pink to red flowers are borne in clusters and made more outstanding by the presence of a small white eye. This is an ideal rose for a pot or tub, where its continuity of flower will be bound to attract comment. In the garden, like all Chinas, it prefers a sunny situation but, unlike some others of its kind, is reasonably happy in poorer soil.
China
1912
Continuous flowering
2 × 2ft (0.6 × 0.6m)

## Stanwell Perpetual

Compared with most roses in the Pimpinellifolia family, this delightful shrub has a long flowering season. Sadly this trait cannot be handed down to any offspring, for 'Stanwell Perpetual' seems to be sterile. The soft, blush-pink flowers are quartered and scented, with soft yellow anthers hidden among the centre petals. Foliage is dark grey-green, with often as many as nine tiny leaflets forming each leaf. Towards the end of the summer the leaves often become mottled with what appears to be a purple brown stain. The affliction, which seems to be unique to this variety, is unsightly perhaps but does no real harm. An adaptable rose that I have seen growing in many situations, 'Stanwell Perpetual' is useful as an informal hedge, good in the border, and very much at home in the wilder garden. It prefers sun and good soil but neither shade nor tired soil will upset it unduly.
Pimpinellifoliae
1838
Continuous flowering
5 × 5ft (1.5 × 1.5m)

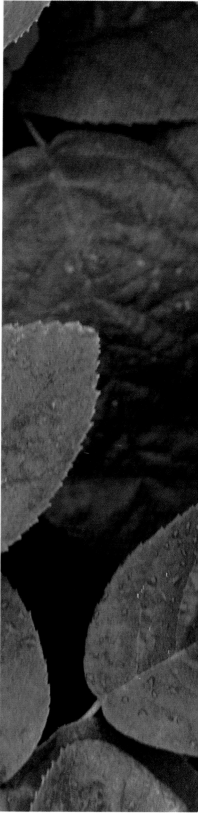

## Rose de Rescht

A beautiful, compact rose with clusters of magenta red, tightly furled flowers that exude strong scent. It is a rose that will tolerate a wet summer. The flower bud is broad and cupped, but with a curiously flat top. Young leaves are paler in colour than their older companions but are finely edged with beetroot red. Very thorny and dense, 'Rose de Rescht' could well be used as a low, formal hedge – shaping by pruning each year will help to maintain its repeat flowering. It is equally happy, though, with other plants in a mixed border or growing in a pot.
Portland Damask (Gallica leanings)
Date unknown
Continuous flowering
3 × 2ft (0.9 × 0.6m)

**Blush Damask**

Little is known of the history of this rose but it is certainly very old. (It is thought that the first Damask rose arrived in England in about 1520. Although some say that the Romans originally introduced them, but that they died out soon after.) Its double flowers have a delightful, though sometimes muddled, formation of petals, those at the centre furling around each other. The outer petals are more relaxed and sometimes curl backwards, to give the impression of a ball. In colour they are mid-pink with lilac shading, fading, as they age, to blush. Although vigorous, this shrub can be rather sprawly. Its leaves are numerous, small and mid-green.
Damask
Date unknown
Summer flowering
4 × 3ft (1.2 × 0.9m)

**Rosa mulliganii**

Until recently this rose has been grown as *Rosa longicuspis*, but its correct name is *R. mulliganii*. The true *R. longicuspis* is rarely seen. Magnificent in mid-summer, this rose has large trusses of single flowers, ideal for nodding from trees and over high walls. Of course, like others of its type, it can also be used for trailing down banks, over mounds of earth, and covering eyesores. Its almost evergreen foliage is dark green, each leaflet being thin and serrated. The younger leaves have a red tinge. The flowers are white with brilliant yellow stamens and a banana-like scent. They are followed later in the year by small, orange hips.
Species
1917
Summer flowering
15 × 10ft (9.0 × 3.0m)

**Bourbon Queen**

Although flowering only in mid-summer, this regally named rose (also called 'Reine de l'Ile Bourbon' and 'Souvenir de la Princesse de Lamballe') is determined not to be overlooked. Its semi-double flowers are almost paeony-like. They are mid-pink in colour and exude a wonderful perfume that lingers in the air. Strong branches arch from the plant and it often needs pruning to prevent it from getting out of hand. If grown as a border plant it will generally settle to the height given below, but planted against a wall it makes a good climber and will get considerably taller.

It is a very useful rose that will tolerate even the worst situations.

Bourbon
1834
Summer flowering
6 × 4ft (1.8 × 1.2m)

**Perle d'Or**

This rose produces masses of buff-yellow flowers, with apricot shadings, from June until October. The flowers are small but when they are fully open the petals fold back in a delightful way. Like most Chinas, 'Perle d'Or' does not have much scent. Its small leaves are glossy, dark green and sometimes bronzy looking, especially when young. Stems are pliable, also bronzy and relatively thornless. 'Perle d'Or' is often likened to 'Cécile Brunner' and certainly it is similar in growth, with the real difference in the flower. A healthy rose, it prefers good conditions and in cold areas will need protection to see it through the winter. It can be grown successfully in pots and is good in a cold greenhouse or a conservatory.

China
1884
Continuous flowering
4 × 2ft (1.2 × 0.6m)

## The Garland

This aptly named rose is impressive by any standards. When in full flush, its numerous, small, semi-double white flowers, sometimes flushed pink, virtually smother the foliage. It exudes the most delightful perfume, which is especially pleasant on a warm summer evening after rain. Its foliage is long and mid-green in colour and its stems are dense, with quite vicious thorns. Untethered, it will reach the top of small trees, will trail elegantly over banks, and, with no apparent effort, cover the tallest wall. Its origin is unknown, but, to judge by its perfume and its inflorescence, it is derived from *Rosa moschata*.
Moschata
1835
Summer flowering
15 × 10ft (4.5 × 3.0m)

## Mrs John Laing

This is one of the best of Henry Bennett's roses. Bennett was the first Englishman to breed good Hybrid Teas but, in the process of producing these, he also secured for us some very good Hybrid Perpetuals. 'Mrs John Laing' is a showy rose producing an abundance of huge, shapely, clear pink, many-petalled, scented flowers. A recognition feature of this rose is the receptacle, which is so small that the stalk seems to disappear into the flower. A healthy plant with large, pointed leaves of grey-green colour, it grows well in most soils but prefers full sun. Its tidy growth makes it suitable for group planting but it is equally at home as a specimen plant or growing in a pot.
Hybrid Perpetual
1887
Repeat flowering
4 × 3ft (1.2 × 0.9m)

**Rosa pimpinellifolia Hispida**
The large flowers of this early-flowering variety are white, shaded with lemon, and display bold yellow stamens at their centres. They are exhibited against masses of small, grey-green leaves very typical of the Pimpinellifolias. Stems are dark in colour and covered in many prickles. Sadly, *Rosa pimpinellifolia* 'Hispida' does not set hips but, if grown with a similar variety of the same species, such as *R.p.* 'Altaica', that does produce hips, it can be forgiven. Early flowering and hardy, it will tolerate shade and poor soil. It is best grown in a large or informal garden.
Pimpinellifoliae
*c.* 1781
Spring flowering
6 × 4ft (1.8 × 1.2m)

**Ferdinand Pichard**
Introduced from France, this (left) is one of the boldest striped roses. It could perhaps be better described as streaked, for each area of colour is irregular and sometimes mottled and marbled. The flowers are largely mid-pink to carmine, with much white. They are cupped and exude a strong scent. The foliage is mid- to bright green, dense, and attached to thick, thorny stems. Grown in the border with other roses it fits in well with paler varieties. It will grow contentedly in poorer ground, but will then probably reach a height of no more than 3ft (0.9m).
Hybrid Perpetual
1921
Repeat flowering
5 × 4ft (1.5 × 1.2m)

**Dunwich Rose**
'Dunwich Rose' (*Rosa dunwichensis*) (top), a procumbent member of the Pimpinellifoliae family, was found growing in the dunes at Dunwich on England's east coast in the mid-1950s. The single, cream flowers, with bright yellow stamens, arrange themselves along thorny, arching branches that give this rose an almost elegant appearance. The leaves are small, mid-green, and numerous. It is only summer flowering, but its hips in late summer amply compensate for this.
Pimpinellifoliae
Date unknown
Summer flowering
2 × 4ft (0.6 × 1.2m)

**Rosa × paulii**
This (above) is an excellent ground-cover plant that will make trailing growths at least three times its height. Its large flowers are pure white and consist of five very elongated petals and bright dusty yellow anthers. Stems are thorny and display coarse, heavily veined leaves along their length. In the autumn the foliage shows lovely shades of orange and yellow. *Rosa × paulii* (*R. rugosa repens alba*) can be grown happily under taller shrubs or trees and will tolerate any shade they may create.
Hybrid Rugosa
c.1903
Summer flowering
3 × 10ft (0.9 × 3.0m)

## Paul's Himalayan Musk

This delightful climbing rose (above) is very vigorous; often, in a good season, it can send out yards of firm but spindly young growth. It is easily trained, but soon gets too big to allow this. Its small, glossy, darkish green leaves are very soft at first and, like those of so many of the Musk roses, tend to droop. Thorns soon develop into tough, vicious protection. The small, double flowers are abundant in mid-summer and are produced in large, hanging clusters. Their colour is soft lavender-pink and, individually, they are very delicate.
Moschata hybrid
Late-19th century
Summer flowering
20 × 12ft (6.0 × 3.7m)

## Blush Boursault

The leaves of this delicate, blush-pink climber (also known as 'Calypso', 'Rose de l'Isle', and 'Florida') are deep green for most of the season, then, long after the flowers have finished, they become beautiful with autumn colours. Wood is thornless, developing a red hue as it matures and also an arching habit. The flowers, produced once only, are flat double and rather muddled. This rose is a vigorous grower, it is good grown on a wall, where it will tolerate poor soil but it prefers to be on the sunny side.
Boursault
1848
Summer flowering
15 × 10ft (4.6 × 3.0m)

## Mrs Oakley Fisher

'Mrs Oakley Fisher' (left) is a splendid continual-flowering Hybrid Tea displaying sweetly scented, large, single, apricot-coloured flowers that form a well-balanced, upright truss. The foliage is dark green and the young shoots beetroot red, as are the many almost-translucent thorns. Flowers, leaves, and shoots together give a very pleasing combination of colours. Growth is compact and upright, which makes 'Mrs Oakley Fisher' useful both for the smaller garden and for growing in pots. It is one of several single Hybrid Teas of the 1920s, most of which have sadly now disappeared.
Hybrid Tea
1921
Continuous flowering
3 × 3ft (0.9 × 0.9m)

## Rosa × paulii Rosea

This (above) is possibly a sport of *Rosa* × paulii, although more likely a seedling. It has the same merits as its parent, among them a tolerance of shade and poor soils. Its large, single flowers of clear rose pink have wider petals than those of *R.* × *paulii* (page 47). A low-growing plant, its long, mid-green branches creep long distances along the ground. They are thick and densely populated with thorns. Foliage is leathery and dark green. Its habit of growth suits it to expanses of uninhabited ground, such as banks and woodland areas.
Hybrid Rugosa
c.1910
Summer flowering
3 × 10ft (0.9 × 3.0m)

**Moonlight**

The result of a cross between 'Trier' and 'Sulphurea', this was one of the first Hybrid Musks to be introduced by the Rev. Joseph Pemberton. Its flowers, of creamy white, are loosely formed, with bold golden stamens and have a delicious musk fragrance. Displayed on long stems of beetroot red, which arch gracefully with the weight of the blooms. Leaves are glossy, dark green, and abundant. The plant is vigorous, tolerant of poorer soils, and does not suffer greatly from disease. It flowers well in late summer.
Hybrid Musk
1913
Continuous flowering
5 × 4ft (1.5 × 1.2m)

**Petite Orléanaise**

As with so many Centifolias, the origin and parentage of this rose (right) are unknown. Although appearing larger in the photograph, the pompon-style flowers are quite small. They are a clear blush-pink, with a tiny green eye in the centre and are displayed against a background of soft green leaves. Other small-flowered Centifolias, such as 'Rose de Meaux' and 'Pompon de Bourgogne' make pleasant companions for this rose but will need to be planted in front of it, for, unlike those two, 'Petite Orléanaise' has growth habits out of proportion to its flowers. Another good companion is 'Petite Lisette', which is slightly deeper in colour. 'Petite Orléanaise' makes a good subject for a pot if its once-flowering habit can be overlooked.
Centifolia
c. 1900
Summer flowering
4 × 3ft (1.2 × 0.9m)

**Charles Lefèbvre**
This very free-flowering rose came as a result of a cross between 'Général Jacqueminot' and 'Victor Verdier', the latter having the Tea Rose 'Safrano' in its parentage. Such a mixture is not uncommon in the Hybrid Perpetuals for they are a complicated race with Bourbons, Portlands, Noisettes, and Teas in their ancestry. The dark green foliage of 'Charles Lefèbvre' sets off large crimson-maroon flowers, which remain scrolled for much of their life. They are held proudly upwards on strong necks.
Hybrid Perpetual
1861
Repeat flowering
4 × 3ft (1.2 × 0.9m)

**Cornelia**
Large clusters of apricot-pink flowers are produced freely all through summer and autumn. The individual flower is small and opens flat, from a rounded bud. The dark green, glossy foliage is tinged with bronze. The smooth, brownish wood is typical of many of the Musks and, with the flowers, makes a pleasing combination of colours. All the Hybrid Musk roses look effective when grown with each other and 'Cornelia' too has proved to be a good mixer. It also makes a good hedge, either on its own or with others of its kind.
Hybrid Musk
1925
Continuous flowering
5 × 5ft (1.5 × 1.5m)

**Conrad Ferdinand Meyer**
This is a rose of large
proportions. Its flowers are
made up of furled, silvery-pink
petals that fade only slightly, if
at all. Their fragrance is
delightful. The wood is tough,
strong, and covered in vicious
thorns. The dark green leaves
are heavily veined and roughly
textured. Sadly, in common
with many hybrid Rugosas, this
variety is rather prone to rust –
and to being attacked by it
rather too early in the season. If
the disease problem can be
overcome, this is a versatile rose
that can be grown against a wall,
as a shrub, or as a hedge.
Hybrid Rugosa
1899
Repeat flowering
10 × 8ft (3.0 × 2.4m)

**Alister Stella Gray**
Large clusters of bloom cascade
from this big, slightly straggly
rambler, whose apt other name
is 'Golden Rambler'. Buds are
small, and deceptively pale
when they first begin to open.
The full, highly scented flowers
are yellow with buff centres and
have a tendency to fade to
cream. The dark green foliage
has a slightly crinkled look, but
is ample and sets off the flowers
beautifully. Stems are thin and
pliable, so the plant can be
easily trained on arches and
trellis. It will tolerate some
shade but in a warm, sunny
situation will do better and give
a good, if irregular, repeat
flowering. This is a lovely, if
slightly delicate, rambler, very
eye-catching in full flush.
Noisette
1894
Repeat flowering
15 × 10ft (4.6 × 3.0m)

**Mary Queen of Scots**
Shown here three times its
actual size, this variety has
single flowers of deep pink
paling towards the centre, with
prominent stamens. They are
produced in large numbers in
late spring on a plant with many
tiny, darkish green leaves and
extremely dark, twiggy wood.
The flowers are followed later in
the season by spherical,
polished-mahogany hips, which
match the stems superbly. This
is an adorable little rose with
many uses; it makes an
attractive small hedge or,
alternatively, is good in a tub,
pot, or urn.
Pimpinellifoliae
Date unknown
Spring flowering
3 × 3ft (0.9 × 0.9m)

**Rosa hugonis**
Although this rose is sometimes referred to as the 'Golden Rose of China', it is in fact more pale primrose than gold. If any gold is visible it is more within the stamens than the petals. It is a large, extremely thorny shrub, covered in small, fern-like leaves of bronze-green colour that turn tawny brown in the autumn after many small dark red hips have been set. Like many spring-flowering roses, it will tolerate shade but will do best – and require little attention – in a sunny, sheltered position.
Species
1899
Spring flowering
8 × 5ft (2.4 × 1.5m)

## Félicité et Perpétue

This is a dainty but vigorous rose, whose rather short flowering period is compensated for by a tremendous display when it is in flower. The small, rounded flowers are creamy-white, tinged with pink, and scented. They contrast with the buds, which deceive by being pink when they first start to show colour. The large trusses of blooms are displayed well against the background of very glossy, dark green leaves, which are almost evergreen. Relatively thornless, it makes an excellent cottage rose as well as being an admirable tree climber. Added advantages are its ability to tolerate north-facing situations and less-than-rich soils.

Sempervirens hybrid
1827
Summer flowering
15 × 10ft (4.6 × 3.0m)

## Dupuy Jamain

The parentage of this lovely rose (above) is unfortunately not known. Fully double flowers of cerise are held proudly on very strong necks and have a delicious perfume. In bud they are plump and pointed but open huge and full, to display many thick velvety petals. The leaves, which have a tendency towards grey in their deep green colouring, cover thick, smooth branches very well, and remain relatively healthy. Its compact yet upright growth allows 'Dupuy Jamain' to grow contentedly in pots or tubs.
Hybrid Perpetual
1868
Repeat flowering
4 × 3ft (1.2 × 0.9m)

## Manning's Blush

The origin and parentage of this Sweetbrier (right) are not known but some Pimpinellifolia influence shows through in its small leaves. It is one of the earliest double forms of the Eglanteria family. The blush-white flowers are large and double, opening flat from rounded buds. They have a pleasing scent. The plentiful, dark foliage is also scented. 'Manning's Blush' does not sprawl in the way that many Sweetbriers do and is easily maintained – all in all, a variety that ought to be used more often.
Eglanteria
c.1800
Summer flowering
5 × 4ft (1.5 × 1.2m)

**Tuscany Superb**
This rose is difficult to overlook
– when it is at its best there can
be few more beautiful roses.
The velvety petals are deep
wine-red with purple shadows;
they contrast strongly with bold
golden stamens and with the
pollen that often covers the base
of the inner petals. The buds are
pointed and surrounded by
feathery sepals. The stems carry
no more than a few thorns. The
numerous leaves are mid- to
dark green and add to the
overall attraction of the plant.
The fact that it is summer
flowering only should not be
held against this lovely rose. It
is mildly tolerant of shade and,
like most Gallicas, will grow
well in most soils.
Gallica
1848
Summer flowering
4 × 3ft (1.2 × 0.9m)

## Prosperity

This is a lovely Hybrid Musk,
sometimes so laden with flowers
that its branches droop under
the weight. It was raised by the
Rev. Joseph Pemberton, the
result of a cross between
'Marie-Jeanne' and 'Perle des
Jardins', varieties still grown
today. Both parents are
considerably smaller in stature
than their offspring but such
occurrences, brought about by
throwbacks to previous
generations, are not uncommon
in rose breeding. As the buds
begin to open a tinge of apricot
can sometimes be seen,
especially in autumn. The
scented, double flowers, borne
in clusters, are white with
creamy centres. This rose must
rank as one of Pemberton's best.
It flowers well into the autumn
and combines well with other
Hybrid Musks. It forms a good
hedge and will tolerate a certain
amount of shade.
Hybrid Musk
1919
Continuous flowering
5 × 4ft (1.5 × 1.2m)

**Mme Grégoire Staechelin**
Introduced by the Spanish
breeder, Pedro Dot, in 1927,
this most distinguished
climbing rose (above) is also
known as 'Spanish Beauty'. Its
double flowers are loosely
formed and have a porcelain-
like quality. The large, pale pink
petals have a deeper reverse and
often, when fully open, a yellow
base. If dead heads are not
removed large urn-shaped fruits
develop in the autumn. Leaves
are glossy, dark green, and
generally trouble free. This
strongly scented rose loves to
spread itself, so is excellent
grown against a wall. It is one of
the few climbers to do well on a
north-facing aspect.
Climbing Hybrid Tea
1927
Repeat flowering
15 × 10ft (4.6 × 3.0m)

**Ballerina**
The flowers of 'Ballerina'
(right) are not individually of
great beauty – they are only 1in
(2.5cm) across, are pink-edged,
paling to white in the centres,
and fade to blotchy off-white as
they age. But, for a mass display
combined with continuity of
flower, this rose is unbeatable.
As if this were not enough, it
combines its flowering feats
with a healthy disposition,
ample foliage, and, not least,
adaptability – it will rise to the
occasion wherever it is grown.
Modern Shrub
1937
Continuous flowering
4 × 3ft (1.2 × 0.9m)

**Cécile Brunner**

A cross between the Tea Rose 'Mme de Tartas' and an unknown Polyantha led to the introduction of 'Cécile Brunner'. Classification is not easy but it is usually considered to be a China. Superb as a buttonhole rose, it has been popular since Victorian times. It is also known, aptly, as 'The Sweetheart Rose', 'Maltese Rose' and 'Mignon'. The irresistible little flowers are shell-pink and delicately scented. They are carried on long stalks in large clusters and give a good continuous display. As a plant it is not easy to grow and tends to be spindly. Foliage is sparse, but this is a fault it shares with several of the Victorian Chinas. A climbing form was introduced in 1894, and another in 1904; these, unlike the bush, are very vigorous indeed and amply foliated.

Chinensis
*Bush* 1881, Continuous flowering, 4 × 2ft (1.2 × 0.6m)
*Climber* 1894/1904, Summer flowering, 25 × 20ft (7.5 × 6.0m)

**Ispahan**

Ispahan, whose origin is unknown, holds a high rank among Damasks. Small clusters of large, clear pink, double flowers appear for a longish period during the summer and these have their fair share of the heady Damask perfume. Buds are round but, because of the long sepals, appear pointed. Leaves are shiny for a Damask and darkish green. Stems do not have over many thorns. Upright growing, it prefers a sunny position.

Damask
Pre-1832
Summer flowering
4 × 3ft (1.2 × 0.9m)

## Mme Plantier

Large clusters of pale cream flowers that fade to pure white are carried on long, vigorous branches. Hidden at the centre of each scented bloom is a tiny green eye, often disguised by the inwardly furled petals. Leaves are greyish-green and held on pliable wood, which does not produce many thorns. The vigour of the plant is variable; it sometimes reaches heights of 15–20ft (4.6–6.0m), but is usually content to stay much shorter. Support is necessary in the best soils. Excellent as a wall plant or climbing into a tree, it can be grown in north-facing positions or in semi-shade.
Alba
1835
Summer flowering
12 × 8ft (3.7 × 2.4m)

## Narrow Water

Pictured here against a wall, this is a versatile rose – not as well known as it should be – that can be grown as a shrub or small climber. The flowers are pale pink, fading with age, semi-double and perfumed; they blend beautifully in clusters with the deeper buds. Small, plain, oval hips follow blooms which go on well into the autumn. Leaves are deepish mid-green, glossy, and narrow for their length. Wood is a chestnut-red. Leaves and wood together provide an attractive background for the flowers. 'Narrow Water' will tolerate shade quite well.
Moschata
1883
Repeat flowering
8 × 6ft (2.4 × 1.8m)

## Claire Jacquier

An extremely useful rose that
occasionally, in good
conditions, will reach to above
average height and give a repeat
performance. It bears clusters of
medium-sized, bright yellow
flowers, which fade to cream
with age. Young blooms tend to
be two-tone, with the outer
petals having already adopted
the paler shade; older flowers
are flat and a little untidy. The
first flush of flowers is always
good, but later repeats can be
disappointing. Foliage is a
glossy bright green, on wood
often tinted with brown. The
vigour of this rose makes it ideal
for climbing into small trees. It
can also be grown with some
success on a north wall, being
one of the hardiest Noisettes.
Noisette
1888
Repeat flowering
15 × 8ft (4.6 × 2.4m)

## Commandant Beaurepaire

'Commandant Beaurepaire'
(right), is, if not the most
flamboyant, one of the best of
the striped roses. The large,
globular flowers are splashed
and streaked with purple, pink,
and crimson and marbled with
white. The first flush is always
excellent and the repeat flowers,
although not numerous, are
usually good. Often the flowers
are hidden by slightly crinkled,
bright green leaves. Careful
periodic pruning is necessary to
prevent the shrub becoming too
thick and untidy. Its dense habit
of growth can make it an
attractive hedge.
Bourbon
1874
Repeat flowering
5 × 5ft (1.5 × 1.5m)

**Mme Edouard Herriot**
The bush form of this rose now seems to be extinct. It acquired its alternative name, 'Daily Mail', by winning a competition at the Chelsea Flower Show just before World War I, when it was also given a gold medal by Britain's National Rose Society. The climbing form, introduced a few years later, is the one we have today. Its stunningly coloured flowers of strawberry coral were unique in the 1920s, but since then such colours have become commonplace, hence its decline in popularity today. The leaves are light green and the stems thorny. The plant demands good soil and its upright growth makes it more suitable for a wall or pillar than for trellis.
Hybrid Tea
*Bush* 1913
*Climber* 1921
Summer flowering
12 × 8ft (3.7 × 2.4m)

## Celsiana

The origin and parentage of this attractive, strongly scented Damask (above) are not known, but it certainly predates the botanical artist Pierre-Joseph Redouté, who was born in 1759. Reproductions of his painting of this rose are well known. Flowers of rich, mid-pink are produced in trusses once each season. They open flat and have bright yellow stamens. Foliage and stems are light green, the older leaves sometimes edged with bronze. Stems are brittle and well thorned. 'Celsiana' tolerates poor soil.
Damask
Pre-1750
Summer flowering
5 × 4ft (1.5 × 1.2m)

## Quatre Saisons

'Quatre Saisons' (otherwise 'Autumn Damask' or *Rosa damascena bifera*) is an extremely ancient variety of Damask Rose. It blooms spasmodically for much of the summer, bearing loose, double flowers of soft pink, with occasional near-white petals around the outside. The flowers are scented and tucked well into the foliage. Leaves are grey-green and softly textured. The plant seems to be happy in most soils, but tends to sprawl slightly – a habit that can be controlled by careful pruning or by support.
Damask
Very old
Repeat flowering
4 × 3ft (1.2 × 0.9m)

## Baroness Rothschild

This superb Hybrid Perpetual (right), known too as 'Baronne Adolphe de Rothschild', is a sport of 'Souvenir de la Reine d'Angleterre'. It was introduced at a time when many breeders were trying to achieve larger flowers and, although this is not the result of hybridization, it certainly has huge blooms. Portrayed against a background of large, shapely grey-green leaves, and held upwards on strong necks, the cupped, soft, mid-pink flowers exude a delicious perfume, which wafts around the garden on warm summer days. This is a good shrub rose, which will tolerate poor soil and settle quite happily into a pot or tub.
Hybrid Perpetual
1868
Repeat flowering
4 × 3ft (1.2 × 0.9m)

## The Fairy

A semi-procumbent rose, 'The Fairy' (centre right) can be relied upon to flower all summer long. Its arching branches carry large clusters of small, many-petalled flowers. These are not scented, but this is a rose lovely enough to manage without perfume. It will not hug the ground in the way of some of the Procumbents, but is low-growing enough to be considered when there are spaces to fill that require a spreading rose. It also looks well, and quite enjoys growing, in a pot. Too much pruning tends to spoil it, as this encourages a certain stiffness and takes away its natural charm.
Polyantha
1932
Continuous flowering
2 × 4ft (0.6 × 1.2m)

## Gruss an Aachen

A good rose of small stature, so that it can be used where space is limited, 'Gruss an Aachen' (right) can, for freedom of flower, compete with the most modern Floribunda. The shapely, very double flowers are cream with an apricot flush in the centre. They fade slightly as they age, becoming soft creamy-white. Leaves are dark green and healthy, forming a good background for the flower.
Floribunda
1909
Continuous flowering
2 × 2ft (0.6 × 0.6m)

## Mme Caroline Testout

'Mme Caroline Testout' (bottom left) is an upright-growing climber with thick branches covered in large thorns. The grey-green leaves make a lovely background for the big, cabbage-shaped flowers, warm silvery pink in colour, which keep their form almost until their petals are shed. It is a climber that can be grown effectively almost anywhere but is particularly good on an archway, where passers-through can pause to admire the texture of its blooms and breathe in its scent. It copes well with poor soils and shade and can be placed successfully on a north wall. It occasionally produces a few extra blooms in the autumn.
Climbing Hybrid Tea
1901
Repeat flowering
15 × 8ft (4.6 × 2.4m)

## Canary Bird

Probably the best known of many similar yellows, this is, as its name suggests, a rose with canary yellow flowers. Thin, arching branches give it a gracefulness out of proportion to its considerable size. The wood is dark maroon-brown, with numerous thorns of the same colour. Its leaves are dark green and fern-like.

Occasionally 'Canary Bird' will produce a flower or two later in the summer. Its arching habit of growth makes it an attractive standard rose.

Xanthina
1908
Spring flowering
8 × 6ft (2.4 × 1.8m)

## Charles de Mills

This rose has large, flat blooms, which, in colour, are a combination of subtly blended reds and purples. The flowers emerge from rounded buds and when fully open are slightly domed and quartered. Sometimes the petal formation is such as to expose a distinct green eye. Like all Gallicas this rose flowers only once, but when in flower the overall display is superb. The foliage is typically Gallica but slightly darker green than most and more heavily veined. There are few thorns of consequence. The dark colouring is invaluable in the garden because it contrasts well with the softer colours of many old roses.
Gallica
Date unknown
Summer flowering
4 × 4ft (1.2 × 1.2m)

## Alba Maxima

This masquerades under a variety of names – it is the Jacobite Rose, Bonnie Prince Charlie's Rose, the White Rose of York, the Great Double White, and the Cheshire Rose. The strongly scented blooms are mostly pure white, but sometimes lean towards cream. They are produced in clusters of as many as eight flowers, all held upwards by a strong stem. Although 'Alba Maxima' flowers once only, the display it gives is excellent. In some seasons, red, elongated oval hips are produced. The foliage is abundant and typical of that of the Albas – a soft grey, it provides an harmonious background for the flowers. In certain situations this shrub can get quite big – the sizes given below apply when it is grown as a free standing plant.
Alba
15th century or earlier
Summer flowering
6 × 4ft (1.8 × 1.2m)

## Complicata

The large, single blooms are bright pink with tints of white at the centre and pronounced yellow stamens; older flowers fade slightly to soft silvery-pink before falling. With leaden green leaves forming a backdrop, this is a delightful rose. It is a good performer on poorer soils and does not object to a little shade. Free standing it forms a large shrub, but if supported, by a small tree for example, it will attain a height well in excess of that given below.
Gallica
Date unknown
Summer flowering
10 × 6ft (3.0 × 1.8m)

## James Mitchell

In mid-summer this well-proportioned shrub is clothed in bright pink flowers that, from mossed buds, open flat with a button eye. The blooms, which have a subtly, refined scent, are sometimes produced singly, but more often in clusters. Moss is present but not dense and is darker in colour than the foliage, which is bright green, sometimes cast with bronze. The accommodating size and tidiness of this shrub permits its use in several differing roles. Content in the shrubbery or on its own, it will tolerate some shade and put up with inferior soil. When in full bloom it is excellent, but it seems sparsely clad later in the year. All in all, though, it is one of the best of the Moss roses.

Moss

1861

Summer flowering

5 × 4ft (1.5 × 1.2m)

## Fru Dagmar Hastrup

More often listed, less correctly, as 'Frau Dagmar Hartopp', this is a first-class Rugosa of the sprawly kind. Used in massed planting it creates excellent ground cover, but it is equally good on its own. It is, though, one of the few members of its family not really suitable for hedging. Its slightly scented flowers are large, single, silvery pink in colour with bold, soft yellow stamens. They are usually slightly deeper in colour in the autumn and are often present on the plant at the same time as large, globular hips. Foliage is heavily veined, darkish green, and of good colour in the autumn. In common with most Rugosas, this rose has an abundance of sharp prickles. It will adapt to most conditions, and as one of the smaller Rugosas, will be content in a pot.
Rugosa
1914
Continuous flowering
3 × 4ft (0.9 × 1.2m)

## York and Lancaster

'York and Lancaster' (*Rosa × damascena versicolor*) is an ancient and somewhat strange rose (left). Its two-toned flowers of blush pink and white vary tremendously, even on the same plant. It is not unusual to find pink, white, and blotched flowers all in the same cluster. They are ragged, semi-double and sweetly scented, with the flowers tucked well into the foliage. Leaves are downy and stems very thorny. The plant is lax in habit and not very free flowering. 'York and Lancaster' may well have been known to Shakespeare. Of interest to collectors and historians but often proves a disappointment as a garden plant.
Damask
Pre-1551
Summer flowering
5 × 4ft (1.5 × 1.2m)

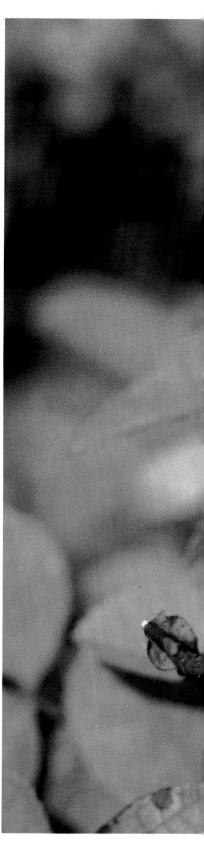

## Thisbe

Clusters of small, flat, buff-apricot flowers appear on this tidy shrub (below) for most of the season, blending well with its mid-green, glossy leaves. Wood is smooth and tinged with bronze. Upright and dense, this is a good choice for hedging. It also makes an excellent shrub for a mixed border.
Hybrid Musk
1918
Continuous flowering
4 × 4ft (1.2 × 1.2m)

## Conditorum

Of unknown origin, 'Conditorum' is an ancient member of the Gallica family. Its rich, magenta flowers are double, loose and muddled in form, and sometimes veined with a deeper hue; the centres display bright yellow stamens. The flowers are scented, but not overpoweringly so. Foliage is dark and plentiful on a bush of upright habit, making it suitable for growing in containers. Like most Gallicas, it will tolerate poor soils and is very hardy.
Gallica
Date unknown
Summer flowering
4 × 3ft (1.2 × 0.9m)

## Scabrosa

The frequent use of this rose by modern landscape architects in municipal and industrial schemes surely says much about its strength and vigour, not to mention its ornamental qualities. Large, rich pink, wing-like petals and bold anthers make up the single flowers, which are followed later by huge, round hips of bright red. The foliage, in common with most Rugosas, is deep green, leathery, and heavily veined. 'Scabrosa' is excellent if used in a hedge but is also well worth growing as a specimen shrub.
Rugosa
1960
Continuous flowering
6 × 4ft (1.8 × 1.2m)

## Alba Semi-plena
The flowers (left) of 'Alba Semi-plena' (*Rosa alba nivea, R. × alba suaveolens*) are abundant for three weeks in early summer. They are semi-double, pure white, and display bold golden anthers. When open they have a ragged look, created by a few random-sized petals curling inwards around the centre. The numerous, grey-green, oval leaves show off the white flowers. Red hips follow the flowers in the autumn. It is a large shrub of loose habit.
Alba
Pre-16th century
Summer flowering
8 × 5ft (2.4 × 1.5m)

## Agnes
The large, buff-yellow flowers of this excellent Rugosa (above) are displayed beautifully against heavily veined, dark green leaves. This feature, coupled with its strong perfume, makes it difficult to ignore this lovely rose, especially as it is one of the few of its type to have any yellow in its make-up. Stems are extremely thorny and growth is dense, making it a good hedging variety.
Rugosa Hybrid
1922
Repeat flowering
6 × 5ft (1.8 × 1.5m)

**Rosa foetida Bicolor**
Bright orange flowers with a yellow reverse are dazzling against a background of bright green leaves. *Rosa foetida* 'Bicolor' is a sport of *Rosa foetida*, to which it sometimes reverts, and it is not uncommon to find orange bicolour and bright yellow flowers on the same shrub. *R. foetida* has passed on its unpleasant odour to its sport, but that should not put you off this flamboyant rose. It can be found growing wild in Austria – hence its other name, 'Austrian Copper' – but it is actually native to Asia. Sadly it is prone to black spot.
Sport of *Rosa foetida*
16th century or earlier
Summer flowering
5 × 4ft (1.5 × 1.2m)

**Schneezwerg**
This hybrid is also known as 'Snow Dwarf', probably because, although it is not small by most old-rose standards, it is slightly shorter that the majority of Rugosas. Semi-double, pure white flowers open almost flat displaying masses of golden yellow stamens around a pale green eye. These are displayed against a wealth of dark, grey-green leaves which change to shades of tawny-gold in the autumn. Hips sometimes set, and when they do are round and bright red in colour, appearing together with the flowers. 'Schneezwerg' is useful in many situations but slightly dwarfed by several of the more vigorous Rugosas. It can make a good hedge. It is tolerant of shade and not averse to poor-quality soil.
Rugosa Hybrid
1912
Continuous flowering
5 × 4ft (1.5 × 1.2m)

**Amy Robsart**
When in full bloom and fully grown, this rose is spectacular. It carries a mass of medium-sized, semi-double, bright pink flowers that fade slightly towards the centre, to meet bright yellow anthers. Although it is one of the Sweetbriers, its glossy, dark green, serrated foliage is only slightly scented. This is a thorny shrub, producing a good crop of oval, orange-red hips each autumn. Like all Sweetbriers, it makes an excellent informal hedge.
Eglanteria
1894
Summer flowering
10 × 8ft (3.0 × 2.4m)

**Harison's Yellow**
This double, bright yellow rose, also known as *Rosa harisonii* and 'Yellow Rose of Texas', is one of many Burnet or Scotch roses and it has a family resemblance to *R. pimpinellifolia*, with its numerous thorns and tiny, fern-like leaves. It also follows that side of its parentage in its habit of growth, which is dense and bushy. It derives its yellow colouring and dark stems, though, from *R. foetida*. An early flowering rose, it will do well in shade and poor soil.
Pimpinellifoliae
*c.*1864
Early-summer flowering
4 × 3ft (1.2 × 0.9m)

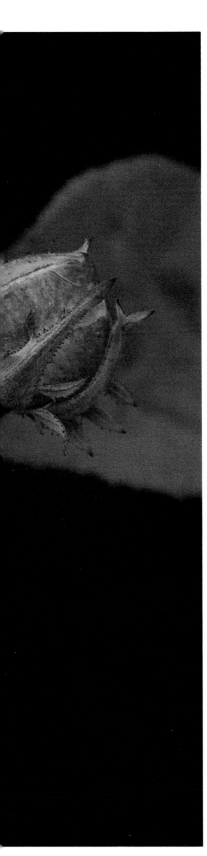

### Duchesse de Montebello

This rose (left) has considerable charm. The flowers are blush-coloured, with deeper pink towards the centre, the petals soft-textured with tissue-paper fragility. It has a lovely perfume. The foliage is dark green, with younger leaves that seem to hang downwards as though reluctant to mature. The bush is upright in habit for a Gallica.
Gallica
1829
Summer flowering
4 × 3ft (1.2 × 0.9m)

### Mme Hardy

The pure white, very double flowers of this rose (right) are strongly scented, large, and compact in structure. Petals fold inwards at the centre, where a bright green eye is visible. The clean-looking foliage is bright green to the eye and downy to the touch. The beauty of 'Mme Hardy' is fleeting – it flowers for just two or three weeks in each year – but despite this it should be seen in every garden.
Damask
Summer flowering
1832
5 × 5ft (1.5 × 1.5m)

### Maiden's Blush

'Maiden's Blush' (right) is a beautiful rose with, it seems, as many names as it has qualities. It is known also as 'Cuisse de Nymphe', 'La Virginale', 'Incarnata', and 'La Seduisante'. The slightly muddled and delightfully perfumed flowers, blush pink in colour, are displayed in abundance in early summer against superb, grey-green foliage. Tolerant of shade and poorer soils, 'Maiden's Blush' is a superb specimen shrub.
Alba
Date uncertain
Summer flowering
5 × 5ft (1.5 × 1.5m)

## Albertine

This must be the most famous of all ramblers. The scented, large, salmon-pink flowers have a charming, rather muddled arrangement of petals. When seen in full flush, it is a stunning rose that fully deserves the accolades it has received over the years. Its flowering season is short but, if mildew can be controlled, the coppery-red foliage is not, in itself, unattractive and, with so few of its competitors any more prolific, this rose will always have a place in today's gardens.
Wichuraiana
1921
Summer flowering
15 × 10ft (4.6 × 3.0m)

## Leda

'Leda' is also known as 'Painted Damask', a name obviously referring to the crimson, brush-like markings on the edges of the furled, pale pinkish-white petals. Each rosette-shaped, sweetly scented flower displays a central button-like eye. The leaves are minutely hairy, soft green, and rounded in shape; immature leaves are russet-brown. The buds show their colour early and then take time to open. 'Leda' is a dense, small shrub, ideal for pot work or placing at the front of a border. Its origin is uncertain. There is also a pink form and one is probably a sport of the other.
Damask
Probably early-19th century
Summer flowering
3 × 3ft (0.9 × 0.9m)

**Baron Girod de l'Ain**
The two biggest attributes of
this rose, a sport from 'Eugène
Fürst', are the size of its blooms
and the strong necks which
support them. The flowers are
globular, with fimbriated edges
to the petals. They are crimson,
delicately edged with white, and
have a slight scent. The large,
leathery leaves are deep green
and attached to strong stems
carrying hefty thorns. The
arrangement of the bush is
somewhat more disorganized, it
seems, than that of its parent.
Unlike many other Hybrid
Perpetuals, 'Baron Girod de
l'Ain' tolerates poorer soil but
in very good soil it is extremely
robust, perhaps growing larger
than the size given below.
Hybrid Perpetual
1897
Repeat flowering
4 × 3ft (1.2 × 0.9m)

**La Belle Distinguée**
The small leaves of this rose are not as strongly scented as those of some other Sweetbriers but nevertheless do have a distinct aroma, especially when crushed. Upright and dense in habit, the plant displays many small, eye-catching, scarlet blooms. Nothing is known about the history of this shrub, except that it is probably very old. One of the tidiest in its family, it makes an ideal pot plant. Alternative names for it are 'Scarlet Sweetbrier' and 'La Petite Duchesse'.
Eglanteria
Date unknown
Summer flowering
5 × 4ft (1.5 × 1.2m)

**Rosa californica Plena**
This lovely rose is a delight. It makes a dense, trim, very healthy shrub, with flowers that are about 2in (5cm) across, semi-double, and loosely formed but shapely. They are lilac-pink and, when fully open, display soft creamy stamens and exude a pleasing fragrance. The leaves are medium-small and grey-green in colour. The wood is light green when young, changing to purplish brown when older. This variety is not densely thorned, but the thorns it does produce are sharp and spiteful. *Rosa californica*, the single form, is native to the United States.
Species form
1894
Summer flowering
8 × 5ft (2.4 × 1.5m)

## Hebe's Lip

'Hebe's Lip' (known also as 'Rubrotincta' and 'Reine Blanche') was introduced by W. Paul in 1912; its origin is not known, but it is thought to be extremely old and probably related to the Damasks. During its short period of flowering, the plant bears an abundance of semi-double, white blooms, delicately edged with red. Its mid-green, toothed leaves are lightly scented. This is a very prickly shrub, with a spready growth habit, and its tolerance of poorer soils makes it an ideal subject in natural surroundings, such as in woodland or at the water's edge. It produces occasional hips and will grow, if not happily, fairly well in shade.
Eglanteria
1912
Summer flowering
4 × 4ft (1.2 × 1.2m)

## Rosa × dupontii

The pure white, delicately perfumed flowers, with sprinklings of pollen from golden anthers, dance in small clusters on a rather attractive shrub. Plentiful greyish, light green foliage displays them to good effect. Growth is also light green and leaf stalks are covered in many tiny prickles. Flowers appear later than many, as does the fruit, which sometimes fails to set. The style of both growth and flowers make this a lovely rose for natural settings and it looks superb in wild gardens.
Species hybrid
Pre-1817
Summer flowering
7 × 4ft (2.1 × 1.2m)

## Comte de Chambord

The large flowers of this upright
and tidy Portland are rich pink
and give off a pleasing perfume.
They are quartered when fully
open, cup-shaped in bud. Petals
are numerous and tightly
packed, with a tendency to be
darker towards the centre. The
buds deceive the eye into
thinking that the flower will be
carmine in colour. Grey-green
foliage is abundant and
individual leaves are rounded,
finishing with a point. They are
an ideal foil for the flowers.
Portland
1863
Continuous flowering
3 × 2ft (0.9 × 0.6m)

**Petite de Hollande**
Masses of clear pink flowers
adorn this shrub in mid-
summer. Borne in clusters, they
are scented and are displayed
well against a background of
mid-green, crinkled foliage.
Petals often curl inwards at the
centre, disguising a tiny green
eye. 'Petite de Hollande', which
can also be found under the
names 'Pompon des Dames' and
'Petite Junon de Hollande', has
a very neat compact growth,
which makes it both an ideal
subject for a pot and good for
mass planting. It can also be
planted with other small
Centifolias, such as 'Spong', to
splendid effect. It is a useful
rose for the smaller garden,
especially if the soil is not very
good.
Centifolia
c.1800
Summer flowering
4 × 3ft (1.2 × 0.9m)

**Mme Butterfly**
There are two forms of this
lovely rose (opposite below).
The bush form was introduced
in America in 1918 as a sport
from 'Ophelia'. The climber
followed, some eight years later,
this time in Britain. Both forms
have been popular ever since, as
garden roses and as cut flowers.
Pointed buds open into shapely,
pale pink flowers that are most
attractive when displaying their
golden stamens. They are
delightfully perfumed and
supported on long necks,
making them ideal for cutting.
Both forms have pale green
foliage. The climbing form is
vigorous and occasionally
produces a repeat bloom.
Hybrid Tea
*Climber* 1926, Summer
flowering, 15 × 10ft (4.6 × 3.0m)
*Bush* 1918, Continuous
flowering, 3 × 2ft (0.9 × 0.6m)

**Mme Lauriol de Barny**
This (above) is a charming
shrub, raised in France, whose
parentage is not known. The
delightfully scented, mid-pink
blooms are borne in clusters
and, individually, are large and
quartered. They emerge from
fat, rounded buds. Leaves are
smooth, mid-green and also
rounded, tapering abruptly to a
point. Stems are smooth and
sport thin, red thorns. Because
it is a healthy plant, 'Mme
Lauriol de Barny' will not
complain too much if grown in
poor soil or semi-shade.
Bourbon
1868
Repeat flowering
5 × 4ft (1.5 × 1.2m)

## Penelope

Another of Pemberton's Hybrid Musks and one of the most popular today. The large, semi-double flowers (above), pinky-cream with slightly deeper shadings, are scented and borne in clusters. Petals are sometimes frilled, adding charm to this lovely rose. Leaves are glossy and often edged with deep red, as are the stems, which are smooth and pliable. Covered in bloom for most of the season, its branches often bow down with the weight of the blooms. Tolerant of shade and inferior soil, this excellent variety will be welcome in most gardens. It will be content in a pot and also makes a good hedge.
Hybrid Musk
1924
Continuous flowering
5 × 4ft (1.5 × 1.2m)

**Max Graf**

Thought to be a cross between *Rosa rugosa* and *R. wichuraiana*, 'Max Graf' (left) was raised in the United States by G. Bowditch. Its stems have the appearance of a Rugosa but its habit is more akin to Wichuraiana. The single flowers of this thorny shrub are produced in summer; mid-pink in colour, they have very bold stamens. The leaves are wide spaced, dark green, and glossy and the mature wood is brownish red. An excellent, trailing, ground-cover plant, 'Max Graf' is quite tolerant of shade. It seldom if ever sets fruit.

Rugosa

1919

Summer flowering

2 × 10ft (0.6 × 3.0m)

**Shot Silk**

The bush and climbing forms of this popular rose (above), are identical in all respects except for size of plant. The sweetly scented, cupped flowers, produced in abundance, are bright cerise-pink and have pale lemon tinges at the base. The plentiful foliage is deep green. The climbing form produces a few less blooms than the shrub, concentrating instead on achieving heights close to 20ft (6m). It will tolerate a certain amount of shade. The bush is slightly more fastidious – it prefers warm situations. It will, though, grow uncomplainingly in a pot. The flowers of both forms tolerate wet weather well.

Hybrid Tea

*Bush* 1924, Continuous flowering, 3 × 3ft (0.9 × 0.9m)

*Climber* 1931, Repeat flowering, 18 × 10ft (5.5 × 3.0m)

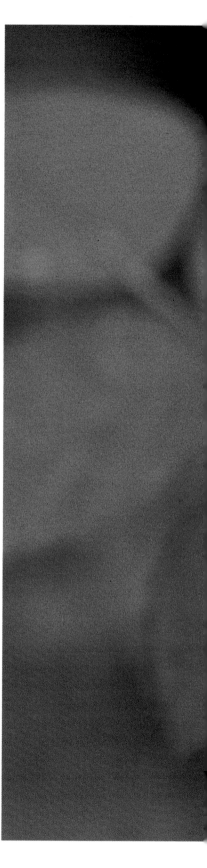

### Easlea's Golden Rambler

This (left) is a healthy climber with ample glossy foliage. The flowers, proudly held by strong necks, are large, well shaped, and golden-yellow, with a pleasing scent. Growth is vigorous and pruning is sometimes necessary. Young growth tends to be copper in colour. Planted beside a tree, 'Easlea's Golden Rambler' will soon mingle with the branches.
Wichuraiana Rambler
1932
Summer flowering
20 × 15ft (6.0 × 4.6m)

### Meg Merrilies

It is possible that this rose (right) is named after the Meg Merrilies celebrated in John Keats's poem about a gipsy woman. It is a prickly shrub that grows large enough to be used as a climber, but its awkward gait prevents easy training. The semi-double, vivid crimson flowers (one of which is shown here twice its actual size) are set off by bright yellow stamens and followed by red hips. Both the flowers and the glossy leaves exude the fragrance of apple.
Eglanteria
1894
Summer flowering
8 × 7ft (2.4 × 2.1m)

### Blanc Double de Coubert

The flowers of this rose (left) are as near to pure white as a rose could be. They are loosely formed and, when open, display orange-yellow anthers to good effect. Unlike many of its kind, 'Blanc Double de Coubert' seldom sets any fruit. Foliage is abundant and mid- to dark green, changing to rich golden-yellow in autumn. It forms a dense plant.
Rugosa
Repeat flowering
1892
5 × 4ft (1.5 × 1.2m)

**Chapeau de Napoléon**

This lovely Moss rose has obtained its name from the interesting formation of moss around the flower buds. The edge of each sepal carries moss that protrudes in such a way as to form the shape of a cocked hat. It is also known as 'Crested Moss' and 'Cristata'. Upon being touched, the moss gives off a pleasing, apple-like scent. The large, double, deep rose-pink flowers have a strong perfume and are cabbage-like in shape when fully open. They are borne on branches that sometimes have the habit of arching to create a sprawly, somewhat ungainly plant, but this can be remedied with support of some kind. Although often grown as a novelty, this rose has much to offer and deserves a place in any garden where space permits.

Moss
1826
Summer flowering
5 × 4ft (1.5 × 1.2m)

**Buff Beauty**
This is a deservedly popular
member of the Hybrid Musks.
Its fully double flowers have a
lovely perfume. They open
from tight buds to become loose
and rather flat. Their colour
tends to vary from plant to
plant, from pale primrose to a
bright, buff orange – a
tantalising idiosyncrasy that
may be due to differing soil
conditions. A minor fault of this
rose is its weak neck for,
although the stems are strong,
each flower bows gracefully
within the cluster, sometimes
obscuring its face. Mature
foliage is dark and glossy but
young leaves are tinged with
bronze. Sadly, they are often
prone to mildew in late summer.
Hybrid Musk
1939 (?)
Continuous flowering
5 × 5ft (1.5 × 1.5m)

## Duchess of Portland

This rose is said to be the original Portland. It may have come from Italy at the end of the 18th century, but opinions vary about this. It was named after Margaret Bentinck, 2nd Duchess of Portland, who was a rose enthusiast. This variety may also be found listed as *Rosa portlandica*, and *R. paestana*). The flowers are only just double; they are rich cerise in colour with white markings in the centre and bright yellow stamens. A short-growing plant with much light green foliage, it is excellent for group planting. It gives a good repeat display of flowers in the autumn.

Portland
*c.*1790
Repeat flowering
3 × 2ft (0.9 × 0.6m)

**John Hopper**
This is a beautiful, delightfully
scented member of its group,
the Hybrid Perpetuals. The
large, full flowers are bright
magenta pink with deepening
lilac shadings towards the
centre, where its petals furl to
give a quartered effect. Upright
in growth and of medium
height, the vigorous plant will
grow well in most conditions
but does not enjoy too much
shade. It makes a good,
impenetrable hedge if planted
about 30in (75cm) apart. It is
also well suited to growing as a
pot plant.
Hybrid Perpetual
1862
Repeat flowering
4 × 3ft (1.2 × 0.9m)

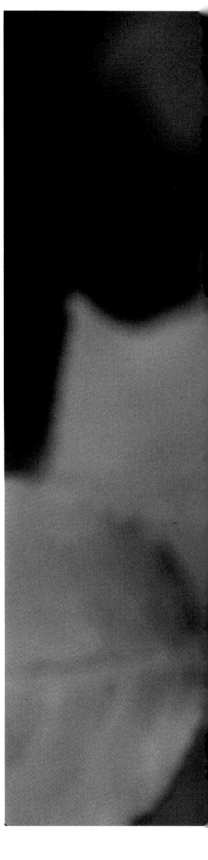

**Alfred de Dalmas**

This (left) is a charming little Moss rose that may also be found under the name 'Mousseline'. Its semi-double flowers are cupped, creamy pink, and perfumed; when fully open they reveal delicate bright yellow stamens in their centre. The ample, mid-green leaves are rounded, with a curious depressed centre and tiny serrations around their edges. The moss around the buds is bright green, with a suggestion of pink that becomes deeper with age.
Moss
1855
Continuous flowering
3 × 2ft (0.9 × 0.6m)

**Mme Isaac Pereire**

The parentage and true origins of this rose (right) are unknown. It flowers throughout the summer, bearing huge blooms, rich deep pink in colour, with a lovely perfume. The smooth, dark green leaves, although of good size, are small in comparison to the flowers. 'Mme Isaac Pereire' can be grown as a free-standing shrub, or it will grow happily against a wall.
Bourbon
1881
Continuous flowering
7 × 5ft (2.1 × 1.5m)

**Le Vésuve**

To thrive, this rose (left) needs a warm, sheltered position; in colder regions it may be better grown as a pot plant under glass or, at least, be given some protection during winter. It also prefers good, fertile soil. At its best, it is very beautiful. Shapely in bud, its flowers, in several shades of pink, are slightly blowsy when fully open. The leaves are dark green.
China
1825
Continuous flowering
3 × 3ft (0.9 × 0.9m)

## William III

The flower of this delightful small shrub is shown here some three times its actual size. In June the plant is a mass of scented, double flowers, which open maroon but fade to magenta and lilac. These are followed by small, mahogany-brown hips. Its numerous tiny leaves are dark green and often towards the end of the season develop small dark splodges. The stems are very thorny. Being compact in habit, 'William III' will grow happily in a tub or at the front of the border, where it will tolerate some shade from taller plants.
Pimpinellifoliae
Date unknown
Summer flowering
3 × 3ft (0.9 × 0.9m)

## Little Gem

A neat and compact, small shrub (opposite below), introduced in 1880 by William Paul, whose rose catalogue listed over eight hundred varieties of recurrent roses in 1884. 'Little Gem', which is also known as 'Valide', displays clusters of pompon-like, bright crimson flowers that recur throughout the season. Leaves are rich green and plentiful on well-mossed stems. It is without doubt, one of the best recurrent Moss roses and is not plagued with as much mildew as so many seem to be. Suitable for group planting, happy at the front of the border and pretty in a pot, this is a very versatile little rose.
Moss
1880
Repeat flowering
3 × 2ft (0.9 × 0.6m)

## Blush Noisette

'Blush Noisette' (above) bears clusters of fragile, lilac-pink flowers, which blanch with age. Its scent is not strong, but this is perhaps forgivable, especially as it flowers in profusion all summer through. The younger leaves are bright green; the older ones, which are arranged in sevens along the brown petioles, are much darker and less shiny. Although it tends to grow rather slowly, 'Blush Noisette' will eventually make a good pillar rose or small climber – or, alternatively, it can be used as a free-standing shrub. Among its merits is the ability to tolerate some shade.
Noisette
c.1825
Continuous flowering
7 × 4ft (2.1 × 1.2m)

## Adam Messerich

This variety (above) was introduced by the German breeder Peter Lambert, who in his time produced several other good Bourbons. The semi-double flowers are rich pink, fading slightly to rosy-pink in strong sunlight; they have a delicious scent and are produced freely in clusters all summer long. The almost thornless stems, which are well clothed in bright green leaves, are pliable and upright growing, giving this rose the versatility to be used either as a tall shrub or as a small climber. It also makes a good pillar or archway rose.
Bourbon
1920
Continuous flowering
5 × 4ft (1.5 × 1.2m)

**Felicia**

This (left) is, deservedly, an extremely popular Hybrid Musk. Its large flowers, of rich pink with salmon shadings, can often be found in such abundance that they almost hide the foliage beneath them. Fading occurs, especially in strong sun, but this has the effect of removing some of the salmon, leaving soft, blush pink. Dark green foliage adorns tough wood, which when young has a bronzy hue. Pruning has no bad effect, encouraging flowers and allowing the plant to stay in good shape. Tolerant of poorer soils it can be grown almost anywhere, except shade.
Hybrid Musk
1928
Continuous flowering
4 × 4ft (1.2 × 1.2m)

**Rosa macrantha**

A rose of unknown origin, although Gallica ancestry is possible. The scented, clear pink flowers (above) consist of five heart-shaped petals that fade to white with age. Stamens at the centre are ochre-orange and surround a tiny green eye. The abundant dark foliage is sometimes tinged with bronze. Rounded bright red hips appear in the autumn, to add a finishing touch. This is an ideal species for the less formal garden, where its arching branches will not have to be restrained. Planted in groups, it makes good ground cover. It will perform well in inferior soils.
Species
c.1880
Summer flowering
4 × 6ft (1.2 × 1.8m)

**Albéric Barbier**
This is an outstanding rambler
raised by Barbier, who was
responsible for producing some
others of our best Wichuraiana
ramblers, including 'Albertine'.
The double, lemony flowers
consist of furled petals of
differing lengths, the shorter
ones tending to remain folded at
the centre. They have a slight
fragrance of apples. A special
feature of this rose is its dark
green, highly glossy foliage,
which remains healthy all
summer and is almost
evergreen. Stems often have a
reddish hue and are pliable
enough to be easily trained.
Although, like most ramblers, it
prefers sun, it grows reasonably
well on a north wall and into
trees, where its tolerance of
shade is an advantage.
Wichuraiana
1900
Summer flowering
15 × 10ft (4.6 × 3.0m)

**Honorine de Brabant**

'Honorine de Brabant' is a vigorous Bourbon variety, strong and dense and almost thornless. It is possibly a sport from an unknown, now extinct, rose. The large, cupped flowers are basically lilac-pink but heavily streaked with soft purple. The plant has an abundance of large, pale green leaves, which often tend to hide the flowers. In addition to making a handsome shrub this rose is a good subject for a wall. It should, however, be kept away from south-facing walls for, in hot sun, the flowers fade and become rather pallid. Flowering occurs over a long period and is especially good in the autumn.

Bourbon
Date unknown
Continuous flowering
6 × 5ft (1.8 × 1.5m)

**William Lobb**
This goes also under the names 'Duchesse d'Istrie' and 'Old Velvet Moss'. The flowers are a mixture of purple and magenta, with some white at the centre and a paler reverse, fading quickly to lavender. They are borne in large clusters on vigorous stems. Leaves are rich green in colour and rather coarse in texture. Buds and young stems are amply clothed in fresh moss, which is sometimes quite sticky to touch. This large, rather straggly plant is better with support, either from neighbouring roses or man-made structures such as tripods or trellis. It also makes a good wall plant, especially if grown with ramblers or with other climbers such as clematis or honeysuckle.
Moss
1855
Summer flowering
8 × 5ft (2.4 × 1.5m)

**Souvenir de la Malmaison**
Another, perhaps more apt, name for this rose is 'Queen of Beauty'. It is indeed a beautiful rose, provided that it is seen on a fine day – in wet weather its lovely, powder-pink flowers become battered and brown, quite unrecognizable. In good soil the best clones of this rose can rise to a height of 6ft (2m) or more but in poor soil it is temperamental and may be content to remain at 3ft (1m). Less fastidious is the climbing form, which should be more widely grown.
Bourbon
*Bush* 1843, Continuous flowering, 6 × 6ft (1.8 × 1.8m)
*Climber* 1893, Repeat flowering, 12 × 8ft (3.7 × 2.4m)

**Empress Josephine**

The Empress Josephine played a major role in popularizing roses in her day. She put together a large collection of rare and beautiful varieties from all over the world and planted them at the Château de Malmaison, near Paris. The rose that bears her name, *Rosa × francofurtana*, was probably in existence many years before and presumably was renamed in her honour. It is a lovely Gallica, with loose, highly perfumed flowers. Its colour is rich rose-pink, with deeper pink veining and highlights of lavender and blush. Its smoothish stems are pastel green, with no more than a few thorns. Foliage is mid-green and made to look coarse by puckering around the veins. It is not too fussy about soil.
Gallica
Early-19th century
Summer flowering
5 × 4ft (1.2 × 1.2m)

**Francis E. Lester**

In full flush, this rose makes a glorious display. Medium-sized, single, white flowers are delicately edged with pink and produced in trusses from arching branches. Bright yellow stamens bring the flower to life. This rose has a nice scent, although it is not as invasive as some. Foliage is shiny and dark green and when young is tinged with bronze. Masses of small orangy-red hips replace the flowers in the autumn. Although vigorous, 'Francis E. Lester' will not take over a garden. It is a superb, under-used rambler, good for festooning smaller trees.
Multiflora rambler
1946
Summer flowering
15 × 10ft (4.6 × 3.0m)

## Rosa gallica Officinalis

This rose, *Rosa gallica* 'Officinalis', has gathered several names over the many years it has been with us. It is the Apothecary's Rose, the Red Rose of Lancaster, the Double French Rose and the Rose of Provins. It was first brought to Europe by Thibault IV, father-in-law of the first Earl of Lancaster, Edmund Crouchback, who adopted it as his family emblem in honour of his wife. The loose, semi-double flowers are light crimson and have a lovely perfume. In mid-summer, this small shrub is a mass of blooms, which do not repeat but are followed by small, roundish hips. Growth is upright and stems are covered with several irregular thorns. Leaves are dark grey-green and dense. Its size and habit make this an easy rose to place in any garden. It will live contentedly in a pot or tub, and in poorer soils. It can also be used as a hedging plant and is tolerant of shade.
Gallica
Very old
Summer flowering
3 × 3ft (0.9 × 0.9m)

## Rosa Mundi

An extremely old rose, surrounded by legend, and thought by some to be named after Fair Rosamund, mistress of Henry II. It is also, more prosaically, known as *Rosa gallica* 'Versicolor'. What is certain is that it is a sport from *R. gallica* 'Officinalis', to which it sometimes reverts. The loose, open blooms are a mixture of violet-pink stripes on a pinky-white background, with a centre of yellow stamens. Leaves are flat, dark green, and heavily veined, although with smooth edges. The stems are prickly with many small thorns. This is a small shrub that can be accommodated in a pot. Although only summer flowering, this is compensated for by the production of fruit later in the year.

Gallica
Very old
Summer flowering
3 × 3ft (0.9 × 0.9m)

# 4

# PROPAGATION

**Budding**

This is the method of propagation most commonly used by rose growers. It requires little parent material and is successful and speedy. At first, a beginner may find the process fiddly and awkward but it becomes easier with practice – experienced budders often propagate up to 400 plants an hour.

A rootstock to make up the roots of the finished, budded rose must first be obtained. These are available from most rose growers. This rootstock should be planted at a slight angle, not too deeply and with the soil banked up around it, in winter or early spring. By the summer it will be ready to accept a bud.

In June, prepare the stock by pushing away the banked-up soil to expose 2in (5cm) of root, then select the scion or bud to be used. Cut a length of flowering stem from a bush, removing the flowers and leaves, and leaving about $\frac{1}{3}$in (8mm) of each leaf stalk. Make sure that this stick of buds always remains fresh, perhaps by wrapping it in damp newspaper.

The rootstock must now be cut to allow the scion to be inserted. A T-shaped cut should be made at the side of the root where the soil was previously banked around it – a vertical cut of 1in (2.5cm) should be enough, with a shorter cut at the top. Now tease away the bark, trying not to split it or damage the stem below it. If you are using a proper budding knife you will find that an area of either the blade or handle has been designed for this purpose. The cut is now ready to accept the bud.

The removal of the bud from the rose stick is a delicate operation. Hold the stick firmly and, with one clean cut, remove the bud. The piece removed should be only about $\frac{1}{8}$in (3mm) thick. With the sliver in one hand put the stick down. The bark and wood below it must then be separated, a process which can be a little tricky.

Holding the piece containing the bud securely between thumb and index finger carefully flick away the soft wood at the base, with either knife or thumbnail, trying not to crease the bark in the process. If the top part of the wood has not come away with the bottom, repeat the process, but from the top or thin end of the sliver. The bud can now be seen, nestled behind the leaf stalk and poking through the back of the bark. Sometimes no bud will be found, in which case a more suitable donor will have to be found.

Much care is needed when inserting the bud. Hold it very carefully at the top between the index finger and thumb of one hand and gently push it into the T-shaped cut, using the other hand to keep the cut open. The bud must be as far down as possible and flush with the wood under the bark. Once it is in place tuck back the bark flaps and cut away any excess bark attached to the bud.

We must now bandage the site of this activity. Rose growers use special rubber patches held in position with wire clips, but raffia is just as effective. It should be carefully wound around the wound, finishing with a knot. After about a month the raffia can then be removed, when it can be determined whether or not the bud has taken. A swollen, healthy bud should be found, often with signs of callous.

However, if this is not the case and it is early enough in the year, another attempt can be made on the reverse of the stock.

The successful attempt should now be left until mid-winter, when everything above the bud is cut away. The cut should be about $\frac{1}{3}$in (8mm) above the bud and left clean. By the following summer a healthy, small rose bush should have materialized. This can then be transplanted, if desired, the following autumn.

## Grafting

Grafting is a skilled job, normally left to the experienced craftsman. As in budding, it involves the combining of the roots of one plant and a scion of another. The choice of stock on to which the scion is put is important, as this will greatly influence the resulting plant. The most common method is 'whip and tongue grafting'.

The stocks are selected early in the year and forced to make root growth by being plunged into damp, sterile peat under glass. When enough root growth has been made the top of the stock is removed, a few inches above the root, in preparation for the scion.

The selected scion is taken from a dormant plant of the chosen variety. It will usually be a piece of one-year-old stem, 3–4in (8–10cm) long, consisting of three or four buds. The top is cut immediately above a bud and the bottom is cut on an angle with any bud at the bottom on the longest side. An upward cut is then made into the scion on the shortest side of the exposed tissue. The scion and stock can now be slotted together, with exposed areas of cambium next to each other. Secure the graft with tape and cover with grafting wax to keep it watertight. Pot up the completed graft, support it with a cane, and keep in a warm greenhouse.

By the beginning of summer, after fusion has taken place and the plant has begun to grow, the raffia can be removed to prevent the plant becoming strangled. After one growing season, the plant should be a reasonable size and can be repotted.

## Cuttings

A rose grown from a cutting does have advantages over those produced from budding. They will have a faster start in life, being able to shoot from each individual bud rather than just the one, as happens on a budded rose. However, they also have equal disadvantages – for a long time the roots will remain small, rendering them difficult to transplant and restricting growth which, although fast at first, is soon overtaken by their budded counterparts.

The best time of year to take a rose cutting is in the autumn, when the leaves are falling and there is ample, young growth available. A cutting should preferably be some 6in (15cm) long and about the same thickness as a pencil; it is also desirable for it to be straight, but much depends on the variety.

Make the lower cut, straight and clean, immediately below a growing point (node). The bud at the bottom can then be neatly sliced away to encourage the development of roots. At the top the cut should be immediately above an eye and sloping away from it to prevent water from settling.

The prepared cutting can then be put straight into the garden, into a trench containing just a little sand, or into a pot in a cold greenhouse or under a frame. The compost should be half sand and half peat. By spring the cutting should have begun to root and have made a reasonable size by late summer. The following autumn it can be transplanted to its permanent site.

It is also possible to propagate roses by means of semi-ripe-wood cuttings. These can be taken from late June onwards and should be prepared from lengths of the current year's growth. They should be only about 4in (10cm) long. All leaves should be removed, leaving only a couple of leaflets at the top. Cuts should be made above and below joints, as for hardwood cuttings, and the base can be dipped in a rooting hormone for speedier root production. The cutting should then be placed in a pot containing a mix of half peat and half sand, well watered, and covered with a plastic bag to maintain a humid atmosphere within. Very little or no watering will be required until the roots are developed in the autumn. Careful hardening off is required, gradually introducing the cutting to a cooler atmosphere until it is ready to be planted out of doors. Different varieties lend themselves to this method of propagation more than others and often a rose produced in this way will be smaller and less vigorous than the same variety produced by budding.

# 5

# PESTS, DISEASES, AND OTHER PROBLEMS

## Pests

### Aphids

Aphids multiply very quickly and can soon spoil a crop of blooms. Regular fortnightly spraying with a systemic insecticide will usually prevent infestation. In days before chemicals, gardeners used soapy water most effectively against these unpleasant little pests. Natural predators of aphids, such as ladybirds, should be encouraged.

### Caterpillars

Several types of caterpillar attack roses. Symptoms are the appearance of nibbling in leaves and in areas of soft, young, succulent stems. Most caterpillars are the larvae of moths that lay their eggs on the leaves or in the soil around the plant. They are more common on roses grown under glass than on those out of doors. Caterpillars are not easy to control. A simple method of eradicating the odd one or two is to remove them with finger and thumb. Severe attacks should be dealt with by an application of derris in either powder or liquid form.

### Cuckoo spit

This little pest is more offensive than harmful. It lives, in its early stages, in a spittle-like froth usually nestling in the joints of young growth or just below the buds. It is at its worst on roses in mid-summer. In the midst of the foam is a young froghopper beetle that feeds by sucking sap from the plant. When it becomes adult it hops from plant to plant, laying more and more eggs. Except in a severe attack, when mild wilting may occur, it does little appreciable damage. The best method of dealing with this pest is to wash it off with a jet of water from a hose pipe.

### Red spider mite

This microscopically small mite can be very troublesome on roses growing under glass. It is rarely found on outdoor plants. It lives on the undersides of leaves and multiplies with speed. The mites cause leaves to become limp and pale in colour, eventually causing them to fall to the ground. Sometimes a delicate web or mesh can be seen on the buds and in the leaf joints on heavily infected plants.

Control is difficult, even under glass. Commercially the mites are controlled by introducing natural predators. The mites thrive in hot, dry air, so a fine mist directed over the plants two or three times a day will discourage them.

### Sawflies

The two most common species of sawflies to attack roses are the leaf-rolling sawfly and the rose slug sawfly.

The leaf-rolling sawfly is by far the most troublesome of the two. The first sign is usually rolled-up leaves – the egg-laying adult fly injects chemicals to make the leaf curl protectively around the larvae when they hatch. As they grow, the larvae feed on the leaf tissue and eventually render it useless to the plant. A seriously infected plant will suffer lack of vigour and become more and more susceptible to diseases. Mildly infected plants do not usually suffer, but curled leaves do look rather unsightly.

Derris in liquid or in powder form is useful in controlling this pest, but other proprietary insecticides are also available. Eradication, however, is difficult, because the curled leaves protect the larvae from the spray.

The yellow larvae of the rose slug sawfly feed on both sides of a leaf, not moving to another until they have left just a skeleton behind. When they are fully fed, they overwinter in the ground in readiness to make a comeback the following spring. If the larvae are seen early enough in the summer, a contact spray such as malathion should be an effective control.

### Thrips

Thrips are sometimes called thunderflies and in dry, hot weather can be quite a nuisance. Individually they are minute and they become visible to the naked eye only in large numbers and after they have inflicted the most damage. They settle on the edges of petals while the flower is in bud and multiply as it expands, causing the petals to become misshapen and discoloured. Mild infestations are not serious, except to exhibitors of Hybrid Teas. If spraying is considered necessary in a bad season, nicotine or malathion can be used as a contact insecticide. Good control is achieved by regular applications of a systemic spray of the type used to control aphids.

## Diseases

### Blackspot

The first visible signs of blackspot are small dark patches on mature, or nearly mature leaves. To begin with these patches are quite small, but as their numbers increase and they gather together they become very unsightly. It is on these patches that spores of the disease develop, usually about a fortnight after infection. These spores then invade the cells of the leaf to sustain themselves and grow, eventually penetrating through to the underside. A single patch can produce many thousands of spores in a very short time. Once the spores start taking nutrients from the leaf it becomes yellow and falls to the ground, where the disease lives on and even overwinters in readiness to spread again the following spring. The loss of leaves from the plant will result in rapid new growth which, in turn, will

become infected, so the bush weakens and eventually dies. It is also possible, in the worst cases, for the disease to attack the woody parts of the plant, producing dark, mottled areas on the bark. Again, spores penetrate into the cells of the stem. Understanding how blackspot spreads makes it easier to understand why it is difficult to control. Removal and burning of all affected leaves and wood will prevent the disease spreading to other bushes.

Spraying as a means of control can be effective but this must be done regularly, before the disease has taken hold. A proprietary winter wash of both the bushes and the rose bed will help kill any spores that may be overwintering on the plant or in the soil. As regards summer spraying, several proprietary sprays are on the market. Some are systemic and these should be used regularly and before any signs of the disease can be seen.

### Mildew

Two major types of mildew invade roses – powdery mildew, the most common, and downy mildew. Attacks of powdery mildew can occur outdoors early in the season, but it normally waits for the warm, dry atmosphere of high summer. At first small spots of a pale grey powder appear on the young leaves and the new, tender shoots. These then spread quickly to flower buds and stems, before moving rapidly to the more mature leaves. In a serious attack new growth becomes deformed and buds are unable to open properly. Flowers that do manage to open are often small and deformed. In addition, a plant suffering from mildew will have a lower resistance to other diseases such as blackspot and rust.

Control of the disease has become easier since the advent of systemic fungicides and regular spraying from April onwards will prevent any spores from getting hold. Contact fungicides are less effective as these are easily washed off by rain. The use of organic mulch such as bark chippings or peat will help, too, by retaining moisture in the soil during hot weather. One sure way to encourage the disease is by the overuse of fertilizers that are high in nitrogen, because these result in excessively soft growth, which renders the plant much more vulnerable to attack.

I have never seen downy mildew on roses out of

doors but it is sometimes a problem in greenhouses and polythene tunnels. Patches of bluey-grey or brown appear on leaves, eventually causing them to shrivel and die. As with powdery mildew, good control is achieved by regular use of systemic fungicides and good ventilation is essential.

*Rust*

Rust can be one of the most destructive diseases to attack roses and some varieties are quite susceptible to this scourge. Symptoms start in early summer, when bright orange pustules appear on the undersides of leaves and, because of their position, often go unnoticed until it is too late for effective control. As summer progresses they become more common, grow bigger, and change colour, firstly to dark brown and then to black. A bad attack will kill the leaves and spread to the stems, causing them to go brown and eventually die back. As with blackspot the spores overwinter, either on the plant or in the ground in readiness to begin again their destruction the following season.

Control is difficult and once the disease has taken hold of a plant the only real remedy is to dig it up and burn it before the disease spreads to adjacent plants. If spotted early enough, infected foliage should be picked off and burnt. One or two sprays are available but these prevent rather than cure, so the secret is to spray regularly from early June onwards whether or not pustules are visible.

*Stem canker*

This disease mostly attacks older plants, especially those that have been heavily pruned over the years. It enters through the wounds left after cutting, especially if the cuts are left jagged or dirty. The canker manifests itself as lesions, swollen in the centre and with unsightly gnarled and dead bark curling round the edges.

The only method of control of bad infections is the complete removal of the plant but, in some circumstances, a measure of control or even cure can be achieved by the amputation of the infected lateral branches and the careful cutting-out, down to clear tissue, of all lesions that are in awkward places. These cuts should be left clean and smooth and coated with a layer of grafting wax.

*Viruses*

Little is known about viruses in roses. Until recently it was thought that they were transmitted by budding knives and the like, but this is now known not to be the case. It is possible, though, that they are spread by insects. Rose mosaic is the most damaging of these diseases; it causes streaking and mottling of the leaves, which eventually turn completely yellow and fall. Growth is held back and flowers open up smaller than they would normally be. The best and only method of control is the removal and burning of infected plants.

Strawberry latent ring spot virus can also occur in roses and the symptoms are very similar to those of rose mosaic. It is transmitted by eelworm and will normally result in the death of the plant. If roses are to be grown on a previously infected site, careful sterilization should be carried out and the ground should be given time to recover.

All this sounds alarming, but most old roses are living happily with a virus of one sort or another and will undoubtedly continue to do so until virus-free stocks can be produced.

**Other Problems**

*Mineral deficiencies and chlorosis*

A rose with an unbalanced diet will usually display chlorosis. This yellowing of the leaves will start either along the margins or the veins, causing them eventually to fall. A deficiency of iron is probably the most common cause of chlorosis in roses. It occurs most often in alkaline soils. A dressing of potash can sometimes help, but sequestered iron, applied in the spring, should correct the deficiency in most soils.

Magnesium is another common lack, which will manifest itself in chlorosis and in misshapen foliage. A solution of magnesium sulphate sprayed on to the foliage or applied to the soil is the best way to correct the balance of this mineral in the plant.

Deficiencies of the major minerals such as nitrogen, phosphorus, and potassium usually show up in the plant as a general reluctance to grow. The soil should therefore be kept in good condition with ample organic material and applications of a good, well-balanced fertilizer at least twice a year.

Although roses prefer a slightly acid soil, calcium

deficiency is not uncommon. This element is needed not so much for nutrition but more as a regulator for other minerals so about 2oz (30g) of lime applied to each rose in spring will often help solve deficiency problems in lighter soils later in the season.

*Spray damage*

These days the possibility of spray damage is ever present in the garden and, when diagnosing a problem, should not be overlooked as a possibility. In the country, wind drift from careless spraying or even a tiny amount of weedkiller from a farm can cause extensive damage to roses. Symptoms of spray damage can easily be confused with other ailments, but the appearance of isolated blotches of yellow on leaves, malformation of young shoots, and disfigurement of flowers are reliable indications of herbicide damage.

# RECOMMENDED SHRUB ROSES

## FOR NORTH-FACING SITUATIONS

### Abbotswood
Canina, 1954
A chance hybrid of Britain's native *Rosa canina*, the dog rose. Its double pink blooms carry a delicious scent. Rather prickly. 10 × 6ft (3.0 × 1.8m)

### Burnet roses
Pimpinellifoliae
These vary in colour and shape of flower but all settle at a height of 3–4ft (0.9–1.2m). Some will set hips in late summer; they are usually chocolate-coloured. Varieties include 'Burnet Double White', 'Burnet Double Pink', 'Burnet Marbled Pink', and 'Harison's Yellow' (see also page 81).

### Frühlingsgold
Pimpinellifoliae, 1937
Very large, golden-yellow flowers appear in late spring. Almost single, they give a beautiful mass display. A thorny plant. 7 × 5ft (2.1 × 1.5m)

### Frühlingsmorgen
Pimpinellifoliae, 1942
The large flowers of this Pimpinellifolia are mid-pink paling towards lemon, and white at the centre. This is a thorny variety that produces its flowers earlier than many roses. 6 × 4ft (1.8 × 1.2m)

### Glory of Edzell
Pimpinellifoliae, date uncertain
Single flowers are clear pink with softer, almost white centres. Early flowering. This is an excellent shrub of upright habit. 5 × 4ft (1.5 × 1.2m)

### Golden Chersonese
*Rosa ecae* hybrid, 1963
Many golden yellow, single flowers are produced early in the season. The flowers are displayed beautifully against masses of fern-like leaves. 6 × 4ft (1.8 × 1.2m)

### Karl Förster
Pimpinellifoliae, 1931
When open, the large, double, white flowers of this rose display bold, golden anthers. Repeat flowering. This is a dense shrub with plentiful light-coloured foliage. 5 × 4ft (1.5 × 1.2m)

### Lady Penzance
Eglanteria, 1894
A more unusual colour of buff, orange, and pink for a northerly situation. Both the foliage and flowers have the delightful Sweetbrier scent. Produces attractive bright red hips in the autumn. 7 × 6ft (2.1 × 1.8m)

### Rosa glauca
(syn. *R. rubrifolia*), 1830
The beautiful, purplish-grey foliage of this rose combined with dark red stems to make it look wonderful in any situation. It will grow extremely well in a northerly aspect. Small, star-shaped, pink flowers are followed by masses of rich red to purple hips. 6 × 5ft (1.8 × 1.5m)

**Rosa × kochiana**

Carolinae, 1869

Small, neat flowers of deep pink with bold, golden anthers. Foliage is bright glossy green and remains healthy throughout the season. A small shrub that copes well with inclement conditions. 3 × 2ft (0.9 × 0.6m)

**Rosa moyesii 'Geranium'**

Moyesii, 1938

Bright red flowers with dusty yellow anthers. These may be slightly reduced in number by a north-facing situation. Large, flagon-shaped hips. 8 × 5ft (2.4 × 1.5m)

**Rosa sericea pteracantha**

Sericea, 1890

Although the translucent quality of the thorns of this rose (also known as *R. omiensis pteracantha*) will not be seen at their best in shade, it will tolerate a north-facing situation. It has unusual, wedge-shaped thorns and its flowers have only four petals. These are white with very delicate yellow stamens. Early flowering. 10 × 6ft (3.0 × 1.8m)

**Roseraie de l'Hay**

Rugosa, 1901

Double, blowsy flowers are a deep, dusky cerise. They are strongly scented and are produced more than once in a season. Fruit sets occasionally and the autumn foliage is stunning. 6 × 5ft (1.8 × 1.5m)

Other roses suitable for north-facing situations are described and illustrated in the colour section. They are: 'Amy Robsart' (page 81), 'Blanc Double de Coubert' (page 94), 'Blush Noisette' (page 103), 'Fru Dagmar Hastrup' (page 75), 'Harison's Yellow' (page 81), 'Mme Plantier' (page 63), *Rosa pimpinellifolia* 'Hispida' (page 45), *Rosa rugosa* 'Alba' (page 34), and 'William III' (page 102).

## FOR SHADED AREAS

**Alain Blanchard**

Gallica, 1839

Purplish-crimson, semi-double flowers display outstanding golden stamens and emit a very pleasing perfume. A compact, dense shrub. 4 × 4ft (1.2 × 1.2m)

**Blanchefleur**

Centifolia, 1835

The heavy trusses of fragrant flowers, white with occasional pink tinges, sometimes cause the branches to bow under their weight. Summer flowering, this rose will also tolerate poorer soils. 5 × 4ft (1.5 × 1.2m)

**Burnet Roses**

Pimpinellifoliae

This little group of roses is useful in difficult areas. Double flowers on tidy plants with many small leaves. Varieties include 'Burnet Double White', 'Burnet Double Pink', 'Burnet Marbled Pink', and 'Harison's Yellow'.

**Chloris**

Alba, date unknown

This rose has darker leaves than most Alba roses. Its double flowers are soft pink and scented. 5 × 4ft (1.5 × 1.2m)

**Gloire de France**

Gallica, pre-1819

Medium-sized, double flowers, deep pink at the centre softening to pale pink towards the outer petals. Fades easily in sun, so is the ideal candidate for shaded areas. 3 × 4ft (0.9 × 1.2m)

**Hidcote Gold**

Sericea, 1948

Single, bright yellow flowers, abundant early in the season. Has broad, wedge-shaped thorns and lots of fern-like foliage. 8 × 6ft (2.4 × 1.8m)

**Mme Legras de St Germain**

Alba, early 19th century

The creamy-white flowers emit a delicate fragrance

and are produced in clusters to give a good display in mid-summer. A large shrub with plenty of good, light grey foliage. 7 × 6ft (2.1 × 1.8m)

## Parkzierde
Bourbon, 1909
Scarlet flowers appear in masses in mid-summer. They are double and only slightly scented and are displayed against much dark green foliage. 5 × 4ft (1.5 × 1.2m)

## Red Wing
Sericea, date unknown
This rose takes its name from its huge, wedge-shaped thorns. Single flowers of creamy-white produced early in the season. Foliage mid-green and fern-like. 6 × 4ft (1.8 × 1.2m)

## Rosa nutkana
1876
Single flowers are lilac-pink and adorn a well-foliated, large shrub. Sets its hips well. In autumn its leaves turn to shades of russet and gold. 6 × 4ft (1.8 × 1.2m)

## Rosa pimpinellifolia 'Lutea'
Date unknown
The single, bright yellow flowers of this rose stand out well in the shade. It has an upright habit, fern-like foliage, and flowers early. 4 × 3ft (1.2 × 0.9m)

## Roseraie de l'Hay
See page 120.

Other roses suitable for shaded areas are described and illustrated in the colour section. They are: 'Agnes' (page 79), 'Blanc Double de Coubert' (page 94), 'Blush Noisette' (page 103), 'Bourbon Queen' (page 43), 'Complicata' (page 73), 'Cornelia' (page 52), 'Dunwich Rose' (page 47), 'Honorine de Brabant' (page 107), 'Maiden's Blush' (page 83), 'Manning's Blush' (page 56), Rosa Mundi (page 112), *Rosa × paulii* (page 47), *Rosa × paulii* 'Rosea' (page 49), *Rosa pimpinellifolia* 'Hispida' (page 45), 'The Fairy' (page 68), 'William III' (page 102), and 'York and Lancaster' (page 76).

# FOR POOR SOILS

## Belle Isis
Gallica, 1843
Double flowers of soft pink with a heady scent are borne in mid-summer amid an abundance of soft, grey-green leaves. A tidy shrub. 4 × 3ft (1.2 × 0.9m)

## Botzaris
Damask, 1856
Fully double flowers of creamy-white, pleasantly scented. They adorn an excellent shrub in mid-summer. 4 × 3ft (1.2 × 0.9m)

## Capitaine John Ingram
Moss, 1856
The heavily perfumed flowers are crimson-purple, fading slightly in strong sun. Stems are well covered with whiskers, which often have a reddish hue. 4 × 4ft (1.2 × 1.2m)

## Dr Eckener
Hybrid Rugosa, 1930
Significantly sized flowers of pale yellow and buff fading with age to lemony-white. Scented. Repeat flowering and very hardy. 10 × 8ft (3.0 × 2.4m)

## Fantin-Latour
Centifolia, date unknown
Very beautiful, flat flowers of mid-to-soft pink with a pleasing perfume. The stamens are often hidden among inwardly furled petals. Foliage is dark green. 5 × 4ft (1.5 × 1.2m)

## Frau Karl Druschki
Hybrid Perpetual, 1901
A strong and vigorous variety with pure white, double blooms. These are displayed against dark, tough foliage. Regrettably without any trace of scent. Repeat flowering. 5 × 3ft (1.5 × 0.9m)

## Fritz Nobis
Shrub, 1940
Although only summer flowering, the large, fully double flowers of this rose are well worth waiting for. They are soft pink with salmon shadings. Hips follow in the autumn. 5 × 4ft (1.5 × 1.2m)

## Frühlingschnee
Pimpinellifoliae, 1954
Large, fully double flowers are white with hints of cream, appearing earlier than those of many once-flowering roses. A very prickly shrub. 6 × 4ft (1.8 × 1.2m)

## Frühlingszauber
Pimpinellifoliae, 1942
Makes an ideal companion to 'Frühlingschnee'. It has fewer petals to each silvery pink flower. A healthy, upright shrub. 7 × 5ft (2.1 × 1.5m)

## Gloire des Mousseux
Moss, 1852
Very large flowers, fully double, mid-pink and pleasingly perfumed. Moss and leaves are both bright green and very plentiful. Summer flowering. 4 × 3ft (1.2 × 0.9m)

## Kazanlik
Damask, date unknown
Highly scented rose used in Bulgaria for the production of attar. Blowsy double flowers are a glowing pink. Summer flowering. 5 × 4ft (1.5 × 1.2m)

## Lavender Lassie
Hybrid Musk, 1960
Lavender-pink flowers in large clusters all through the summer months, fully double and opening flat. Continuous flowering. 5 × 4ft (1.5 × 1.2m)

## Mme de Tartas
Tea, 1859
One of the few Tea Roses to tolerate poorer soils. The large, fully double flowers are soft pink and scented. Continuous flowering. 3 × 3ft (0.9 × 0.9m)

## Miss Edith Cavell
Polyantha, 1917
This is an attractive little rose, of small, neat habit, bearing large trusses of scarlet, semi-double flowers. Continuous flowering. 2 × 2ft (0.6 × 0.6m)

## Mrs Colville
Pimpinellifoliae, date unknown
Flowers are small, single, deep velvety red seeming almost purple in some lights. Bright golden anthers surround a conspicuous white eye. Foliage is fern-like on dark mahogany wood. Hips appear in the autumn. 4 × 3ft (1.2 × 0.9m)

## Mutabilis
China, 1932
The flowers of this China are out of the ordinary and are, in their own way, beautiful. They are single and, in colour, a combination of yellow, pink, peach, and red. 3 × 2ft (0.9 × 0.6m)

## Nevada
Possible hybrid of *Rosa moyesii*, 1927
A beautiful rose with large, blowsy, almost single creamy-white flowers with golden-orange stamens. The first, stunning flush is usually fairly early and is followed by intermittent flowers as the season progresses. 8 × 7ft (2.4 × 2.1m)

## Nuits de Young
Moss, 1845
Very dark, velvety maroon petals are enhanced by bright golden stamens. Leaves smaller than many in this group. Dark, mossy stems. 4 × 3ft (1.2 × 0.9m)

## Robin Hood
Hybrid Musk, 1927
Flowers either single or double, scarlet-crimson, of medium size and produced in large clusters all summer long. 4 × 3ft (1.2 × 0.9m)

## Rose d'Amour
*Rosa virginiana plena*, pre-1820
Beautiful flowers of mid-pink remain scrolled for most of their life. Plants of this variety can get much taller than suggested below if well fed and grown on a wall but in poor soil they are likely to reach maturity rather slowly. 7 × 5ft (2.1 × 1.5m)

## Vanguard
Rugosa, 1932
A substantial shrub with large, fully double flowers of salmon-pink. Highly scented. 8 × 6ft (2.4 × 1.8m)

Other roses that tolerate poorer soils are described and illustrated in the colour section. They are: 'Alba

Maxima' (page 71), 'Baron Girod de l'Ain' (page 85), 'Bourbon Queen' (page 43), 'Buff Beauty' (page 97), 'Celsiana' (page 67), 'Charles de Mills' (page 71), 'Duchess of Portland' (page 98), 'Duchesse de Montebello' (page 83), 'Felicia' (page 105), 'Honorine de Brabant' (page 107), 'Leda' (page 84), 'Mme Hardy' (page 83), 'Narrow Water' (page 63), Rosa Mundi (page 112), and 'William Lobb' (page 108).

## FOR HEDGING

### Autumn Fire ('Herbstfeuer')
Eglanteria Hybrid, 1961
Large flowers are dark red, semi-double, and fragrant and they are produced for most of the season. These are superseded by large, orange hips in the autumn. Ideal for an informal hedge. 6 × 4ft (1.8 × 1.2m)

### Burnet Roses
Pimpinellifoliae
All the members of this little group are compact and prickly, ideal for shorter hedges. Varieties include 'Burnet Double Pink', 'Burnet Marbled Pink', 'Burnet Double White', and 'Harison's Yellow'.

### Cardinal de Richelieu
Gallica, 1840
Rich velvety purple flowers, well perfumed and displayed against abundant mid-green leaves. This rose makes an ideal shorter hedge on its own but it also mixes very well with other Gallicas. 4 × 3ft (1.2 × 0.9m)

### Carmen
Rugosa, 1907
Large, single flowers of dark crimson with a velvety texture to the petals, set off by pronounced golden stamens when open, Although it only sets fruit now and then it has excellent autumn foliage. 5 × 4ft (1.5 × 1.2m)

### Celestial
Alba, date unknown
Beautiful, semi-double, soft pink flowers, heavily perfumed, superbly set amongst grey-green leaves. A very healthy rose and quite dense. 5 × 3ft (1.5 × 0.9m)

### Erfurt
Modern Shrub, 1939
Almost single flowers of deep rosy pink paling towards a white eye at the centre, where bold ochre anthers are prominent. Creates a fantastic display as a hedge and will tolerate pruning well. 5 × 4ft (1.5 × 1.2m)

## Fimbriata
Rugosa, 1891
Small rosette-like flowers with tattered edges, their soft pink colouring fading to white with age. A lovely rose with ample, tough, bright green foliage. 4 × 4ft (1.2 × 1.2m)

## Francesca
Hybrid Musk, 1928
Semi-double, apricot to yellow flowers produced continuously throughout the season. Foliage is glossy, dark green and, with the stems, makes a pleasing foil to the flowers. Withstands hard pruning to create a formal hedge. 4 × 4ft (1.2 × 1.2m)

## Frühlingsmorgen
See page 119.

## Gloire Lyonnaise
Hybrid Perpetual, 1885
Semi-double, creamy-white flowers are well scented and held proudly on strong necks. Dark green foliage suits the colour of the flowers. Its upright growth makes it ideal for a formal hedge. 4 × 2ft (1.2 × 0.6m)

## Henri Martin
Moss, 1863
In mid-summer this variety is covered with masses of double, scented, crimson flowers. May need cutting back to maintain an orderly hedge but ideal if left to develop its own personality. 5 × 4ft (1.5 × 1.2m)

## Ipsilante
Gallica, 1829
Quartered pale pink flowers exude a lovely perfume. Foliage green, stems thorny. If pruned after flowering each year this rose makes the ideal, semi-informal hedge. 4 × 3ft (1.2 × 0.9m)

## Mrs Anthony Waterer
Rugosa, 1898
The double, rich crimson flowers are scented and provide a continuous display. Makes a very dense, thorny hedge. Mildew needs watching in dry seasons. 4 × 5ft (1.2 × 1.5m)

## Nuits de Young
See page 122.

## Paul Neyron
Hybrid Perpetual, 1869
Huge, rich pink flowers, fully double and pleasantly scented. These are borne on a strong, healthy plant with dark green leaves. Will not enjoy too much shade. 3 × 2ft (0.9 × 0.6m)

## Pink Prosperity
Hybrid Musk, 1931
Small flowers of clear pink appear in clusters throughout the season. This rose has dark, glossy leaves and a fairly upright habit. Denser in growth than most Hybrid Musks. 4 × 4ft (1.2 × 1.2m)

## Pompon Blanc Parfait
Alba, c.1867
A tidy plant with an upright habit. Pure white flowers appear in large clusters in mid-summer and are pleasingly perfumed. Has few thorns. 4 × 3ft (1.2 × 0.9m)

## Rosa × micrugosa 'Alba'
Date unknown
Large, silky textured, single flowers of pure white with bold yellow anthers, produced with regularity throughout the season on a dense, well-foliated, Rugosa-like shrub. Globular orange hips in the autumn. 5 × 4ft (1.5 × 1.2m)

## Rose de Meaux
Centifolia, pre-1789
A short, tidy hedge can be achieved with this dainty Centifolia. Its small double flowers are soft pink and appear abundantly in June. There is also a white form that can be mixed with the pink to make an interesting hedge. 2 × 2ft (0.6 × 0.6m)

## Salet
Moss, 1854
Double flowers of clear pink adorn a plant with bright green leaves and mossed stems. Will produce more than one flush each season. 4 × 3ft (1.2 × 0.9m)

Other roses that make good hedges are described

and illustrated in the colour section. They are: 'Agnes' (page 79), 'Alba Maxima' (page 71), 'Alba Semi-plena' (page 79), 'Ballerina' (page 60), 'Belle Poitevine' (page 36), 'Blanc Double de Coubert' (page 94), 'Buff Beauty' (page 97), 'Canary Bird' (page 70), 'Charles de Mills' (page 71), 'Comte de Chambord' (page 88), 'Cornelia' (page 52), 'Duchess of Portland' (page 98), 'Felicia' (page 105), 'Mme Plantier' (page 63), 'Maiden's Blush' (page 83), 'Manning's Blush' (page 56), 'Moonlight' (page 50), 'Penelope' (page 92), 'Prosperity' (page 59), Rosa Mundi (page 112), 'Rose de Rescht' (page 40), and 'Stanwell Perpetual' (page 40).

## FOR THE SMALLER GARDEN

### Angèle Pernet
Hybrid Tea, 1924
Orange-yellow, perfumed flowers, carried on a tidy plant, are displayed against very dark green foliage. Continuous flowering. 2 × 2ft (0.6 × 0.6m)

### Burnet Roses
Pimpinellifoliae
All the Burnet roses are well suited to smaller gardens.

### Camaieux
Gallica, 1830
Fully double blooms have stripes of deep pink and purplish-crimson on a background of soft blush pink. A tidy plant. 3 × 3ft (0.9 × 0.9m)

### Cameo
Polyantha, 1932
Small flowers are fully double, soft salmon-pink, and borne in large clusters. Continuous flowering. 2 × 2ft (0.6 × 0.6m)

### Deuil de Paul Fontaine
Moss, 1873
Very dark red flowers appear at first in profusion and then intermittently throughout the summer. Foliage is tough, dark green. 3 × 3ft (0.9 × 0.9m)

### Golden Melody
Hybrid Tea, 1934
The scented flowers of this rose are shapely, golden yellow with occasional buff and pink shadows. Ideal for cutting. Continuous flowering. 3 × 2ft (0.9 × 0.6m)

### Golden Salmon Superior
Polyantha, 1926
Small, salmon-orange flowers cover this small bush for a long period. An excellent rose, quite happy if planted with others of its kind. 2 × 2ft (0.6 × 0.6m)

### Irène Watts
China, 1896
Large, double flowers are peachy-pink with stronger

shadings, often appearing too big for such a tiny shrub. Leaves are dark green. 2 × 2ft (0.6 × 0.6m)

## Jacques Cartier
Portland, 1868
Pink flowers are almost rosette-shaped, with edges that appear frilled. Highly scented and gives a continuous display. 3 × 2ft (0.9 × 0.6m)

## Lady Hillingdon
Climbing Tea, 1910
Flowers are a useful colour – a clear orangy-yellow. Highly perfumed and displayed against dark green, polished leaves. Continuous flowering, but prefers a warm, sunny situation. 3 × 2ft (0.9 × 0.6m)

## La Reine
Hybrid Perpetual, 1842
Lilac-to-pink petals form cupped flowers borne on long, upright, well-foliated stems. Continuous flowering. 3 × 2ft (0.9 × 0.6m)

## Louis XIV
China, 1859
Very rich, deep red almost black flowers open to reveal golden stamens. A loosely formed plant with very few thorns. Continuous throughout the summer. 2 × 2ft (0.6 × 0.6m)

## Miss Edith Cavell
See page 122.

## Pompon de Bourgogne
Centifolia, pre-1664
The colour of the flowers is somewhere between deep pink and purple. They are small and produced in abundance on an excellent little shrub. Summer flowering. 2 × 2ft (0.6 × 0.6m)

## Queen of Bedders
Bourbon, 1871
Not very well known, this rose hardly ever lives up to its name when grown among other plants, but on its own it has much to offer. The flowers are a deep carmine colour fading slightly with age and are produced throughout the season. 3 × 2ft (0.9 × 0.6m)

## Rose de Meaux
See page 124.

## Rose d'Hivers
Damask, date unknown
Flowers are white with pink overtones, displayed against leaves of greyish-green. Repeat flowering. 3 × 3ft (0.9 × 0.9m)

## Rose du Roi à Fleurs Pourprés
Portland, 1819
A bushy shrub bearing flowers of deep violet-red. A very useful colour with white and creams. 3 × 3ft (0.9 × 0.9m)

## Single Cherry
Pimpinellifoliae, date unknown
An early flowering rose bearing masses of small, single, cherry-red flowers. These are set off by an abundance of tiny, dark leaves. Produces small, black hips in the autumn. 3 × 3ft (0.9 × 0.9m)

## White Pet
Dwarf Sempervirens, 1879
The flowers are almost identical to those of 'Félicité et Perpétue', from which this little rose sported, being small, double, and white. Very dark green, glossy foliage. 2 × 2ft (0.6 × 0.6m)

More roses suitable for the smaller garden are described and illustrated in the colour section. They are: 'Blush Noisette' (page 103), 'Duchess of Portland' (page 98), 'Gruss an Aachen' (page 68), 'Le Vésuve' (page 100), 'Little Gem' (page 102), 'Mrs Oakley Fisher' (page 49), 'Perle d'Or' (page 43), Rosa Mundi (page 112), 'Rose de Rescht' (page 40), 'Souvenir de la Malmaison' (page 108), 'The Fairy' (page 68), and 'William III' (page 102).

## FOR TUBS AND POTS

### Blanc de Vibert
Portland, 1847
Large, white flowers with lemon tinges at the centre. Fully double, they have a wonderful perfume and are displayed against a background of matt green leaves. Repeat flowering. 3 × 3ft (0.9 × 0.9m)

### Burnet Roses
See page 119.

### Eugène Fürst
Hybrid Perpetual, 1875
Very deep crimson-purple flowers are superbly perfumed and borne proudly against lush, green leaves. A lovely, deeply coloured rose, probably best in a largish tub. Its striped sport, 'Baron Girod de l'Ain', is also good. Repeat flowering. 4 × 3ft (1.2 × 0.9m)

### Georges Vibert
Centifolia, 1853
The compactness of this rose makes it one of the best striped varieties for growing in a tub. Colour varies from a combination of mid-pink to mauve. Good foliage, but only once flowering. 3 × 3ft (0.9 × 0.9m)

### Hermosa
China, 1840
Full, cupped flowers of soft mid-pink appear regularly throughout the summer. It does well even in a smaller tub. 3 × 2ft (0.9 × 0.6m)

### Horstmann's Rosenresli
Floribunda, 1955
The scented flowers, borne in clusters, are creamy-white and full. They are produced all summer against an abundance of fresh green leaves. 3 × 2ft (0.9 × 0.6m)

### Louis XIV
See page 126.

### Mme Pierre Oger
Bourbon, 1878
Cupped flowers formed from delicate petals of pale pink, often with deeper shades at the edges and always beautifully perfumed. A medium-sized bush seldom without flowers. Needs watching for black spot. 4 × 4ft (1.2 × 1.2m)

### Mme de Tartas
See page 122.

### Ma Ponctuée
Moss, 1857
An ideal subject for a pot. May need a little extra attention to give of its best, which is excellent. The pinkish-white flowers often display tiny white flecks. 3 × 3ft (0.9 × 0.9m)

### Nanette
Centifolia, date unknown
Brightly coloured flowers with a background of crimson and purple blotches. A compact shrub with dark green foliage and few thorns of consequence. 3 × 3ft (0.9 × 0.9m)

### Omar Khayyam
Damask, 1839
This is an interesting rose. It originally came from seeds growing at the tomb of Omar Khayyam in Nashipur. The flowers are mid-pink, double, and scented. Summer flowering. 3 × 3ft (0.9 × 0.9m)

### Pélisson
Moss, 1948
Double flowers of magenta red change to purple as they become older. The leaves and moss are dark green. Summer flowering. 4 × 3ft (1.2 × 0.9m)

### Rose du Roi
Portland, 1815
The flowers are red, sometimes overcast with purple, and reflex neatly towards the centre. Highly perfumed. 3 × 3ft (0.9 × 0.9m)

### Spong
Centifolia, 1805
Upright growing and well foliated, this variety is adorned with masses of small, soft pink flowers in mid-summer. Slightly scented. Do not let the unusual name put you off. 4 × 3ft (1.2 × 0.9m)

## Variegata di Bologna

Bourbon, 1909

Off-white blotched and striped with purple. Repeat flowering. 6 × 5ft (1.8 × 1.5m)

## White Grootendorst

Rugosa, 1962

The pure white flowers are small and rosette-shaped (rather like Dianthus). They appear in clusters on a tough, prickly shrub all summer through. 4 × 3ft (1.2 × 0.9m)

## William R. Smith

Tea, 1909

Loosely formed flowers are cream with a faint pink shading and have tinges of gold towards the centre. Repeat flowering. 3 × 2ft (0.9 × 0.6m)

Other roses that are good in pots are described and illustrated in the colour section. They are: 'Alfred de Dalmas' (page 100), 'Ballerina' (page 60), 'Comte de Chambord' (page 88), 'Duchesse de Montebello' (page 83), 'Dunwich Rose' (page 47), 'Felicia' (page 105), 'Gruss an Aachen' (page 68), 'Leda' (page 84), 'Little Gem' (page 102), 'Papa Hémeray' (page 39), Rosa Mundi (page 112), 'Rose de Rescht' (page 40), 'Souvenir de la Malmaison' (page 108), 'The Fairy' (page 68), and 'William III', (page 102).

# FOR GREENHOUSE AND CONSERVATORY

## Clementina Carbonieri

Tea, 1913

The colour is a blend of mustard yellow, coral-pink, and red, striking against a background of dark green leaves. 3 × 2ft (0.9 × 0.6m)

## Comtesse du Cayla

China, 1902

Vivid flowers, almost single, of bright orangy-pink. Highly perfumed. Very free flowering. 3 × 3ft (0.9 × 0.9m)

## Duchesse de Brabant

Tea, 1857

Flowers are loosely double, clear pink, and strongly scented. They are produced on a well-foliated, wildish-growing plant. This variety does exceptionally well under glass. 3 × 3ft (0.9 × 0.9m)

## Mme Bravy

Tea, 1846

Flowers are large, creamy-white with a pink blush, and are well perfumed. Produced continuously throughout the summer on a tidy-growing plant. 3 × 2ft (0.9 × 0.6m)

## Mme Jules Gravereaux

Tea, 1901

The pale buff flowers with pink and peachy shadings are fully double. A pleasing colour combination against dark green leaves and even darker stems. A shorter climber that will appreciate being grown under glass. 8 × 6ft (2.4 × 1.8m)

## Ophelia

Hybrid Tea, 1912

In the 1920s and 1930s this rose was grown under glass commercially. The flowers are beautifully formed, soft pink in colour, and delightfully perfumed. 3 × 2ft (0.9 × 0.6m)

## Papillon

China, 1900

A lovely rose with loose flowers of coral-pink displaying tinges of yellow. These are portrayed against dark, glossy leaves. Continuous flowering. 2 × 2ft (0.6 × 0.6m)

## Perle des Jardins

Tea, 1874

Clear yellow flowers, fully double, large and scented. Growth neat and tidy. Ample good mid-green foliage. 3 × 2ft (0.9 × 0.6m)

## The Bride

Tea, 1885

Pure white petals sometimes tinged with pink make up the beautifully formed flowers of this rose. A good-sized, vigorous plant with lush foliage. 4 × 3ft (1.2 × 0.9m)

Two other roses that are good under glass are described and illustrated in the colour section. They are 'Le Vésuve' (page 100), and 'Perle d'Or' (page 43).

## FOR THE SCENTED GARDEN

## Amélia

Alba, 1823

Superbly perfumed, semi-double flowers of mid-pink, with golden anthers, against a background of softly textured, grey-green leaves. 4 × 3ft (1.2 × 0.9m)

## Anne of Geierstein

Sweetbrier, 1894

Single flowers of crimson-red with a discreet yellow splash at the centre. Both flowers and foliage well scented. 10 × 8ft (3.0 × 2.4m)

## Belle de Crécy

Gallica, mid 19th century

The quartered flowers are a pleasant combination of pale pink and mauve, lovely colouring to accompany greyish-green foliage. Very highly perfumed. A tidy, upright shrub. 4 × 3ft (1.2 × 0.9m)

## Blanche de Belgique

Alba, 1817

Flowers of pure white transmitting the distinctive, refined, Alba perfume. An upright, healthy shrub with lots of grey-green foliage. 6 × 4ft (1.8 × 1.2m)

## Capitaine John Ingram

See page 121.

## Duc de Guiche

Gallica, 1835

Large, double, violet-pink flowers that, when fully open, expose a curious central green eye. Very similar in most respects except colour to 'Charles de Mills'. 4 × 4ft (1.2 × 1.2m)

## Gloire de Guilan

Damask, 1949

This variety was commonly used in the extraction of rose attar. The flowers are clear pink and quartered and produced on a good, well-foliated plant. 6 × 4ft (1.8 × 1.2m)

## Jacques Cartier

See page 126.

## Juno

Gallica, 1832

A shrub with a graceful, arching habit. Flowers of pale pink produced in masses, emitting a fine fragrance. 4 × 4ft (1.2 × 1.2m)

## Kazanlik

See page 122.

## Königin von Dänemark

Alba, 1826

Rosette-shaped flowers of blush pink fading only slightly with age. Upright and healthy in habit. Superb perfume. 5 × 4ft (1.5 × 1.2m)

## Mme Knorr

Portland, 1855

A compact, tidy shrub displaying semi-double, bright pink flowers with a superb fragrance. 3 × 3ft (0.9 × 0.9m)

## Paul Neyron

See page 124.

## Réné d'Anjou

Moss, 1853

The very delicate, pink flowers are highly perfumed and give a good display in June. A compact shrub with soft green foliage which, when young, is tinged red. 4 × 3ft (1.2 × 0.9m)

Other roses that are, to a greater or lesser degree, scented are described and illustrated in the colour section. They are: 'Agnes' (page 79), 'Alba Maxima' (page 71), 'Baroness Rothschild' (page 68), 'Buff Beauty' (page 97), 'Celsiana' (page 67), 'Charles de Mills' (page 71), 'Comte de Chambord' (page 88), 'Duchess of Portland' (page 98), 'Duchesse de Montebello' (page 83), 'Dupuy Jamain' (page 56), 'Felicia' (page 105), 'Hebe's Lip' (page 87), 'Ispahan' (page 62), 'Louise Odier' (page 38), 'Mme Hardy' (page 83), 'Mme Isaac Pereire' (page 100), 'Maiden's Blush' (page 83), 'Manning's Blush' (page 56), 'Mrs John Laing' (page 44), 'Mrs Oakley Fisher' (page 49), 'Penelope' (page 92), 'Quatre Saisons' (page 67), and 'Souvenir de la Malmaison' (page 108).

# RECOMMENDED CLIMBERS AND RAMBLERS

## FOR NORTH-FACING SITUATIONS

**Bleu Magenta**
Multiflora rambler, c. 1900
Royal purple petals surround golden stamens. Sweetly perfumed flowers appear en masse in mid-summer. Might get a little mildew after flowering on otherwise good foliage. 12 × 10ft (3.7 × 3.0 m)

**Bobbie James**
Multiflora rambler, 1961
Fresh green leaves provide a good foil for heavy trusses of semi-double, creamy flowers, which exude a pleasant scent. These are succeeded by good hips. Foliage turns to shades of yellow in the autumn. Very healthy even in shade. 30 × 20ft (9.0 × 6.0m)

**Climbing Mrs Herbert Stevens**
Hybrid Tea, 1910
A beautiful climber with shapely white flowers and a delightful scent. A very popular rose in the first half of this century. 12 × 8ft (3.7 × 2.4m)

**Crimson Conquest**
Hybrid Tea, 1931
Semi-double, rich crimson flowers are carried on a well-foliated, healthy plant. Summer flowering. 15 × 8ft (4.6 × 2.4m)

**Emily Gray**
Wichuraiana, 1918
Healthy, glossy foliage makes a perfect backdrop for blowsy, yellow flowers. Semi-double. Perfumed. 15 × 10ft (4.6 × 3.0m)

**Evangeline**
Wichuraiana, 1906
Produces one flush of flowers slightly later than those of many other summer-flowering roses. They are single, pinkish-white, borne in trusses. Shiny, leathery foliage. 15 × 12ft (4.6 × 3.7m)

**François Juranville**
Wichuraiana, 1906
Clear pink flowers are fully double and make a wonderful spectacle in mid-summer. Young wood has a bronzy tinge. 12 × 10ft (3.7 × 3.0m)

**Ghislaine de Féligonde**
Multiflora rambler, 1916
A small rambler with double, apricot-yellow flowers that appear in more than one showing each season. Virtually thornless. 8 × 8ft (2.4 × 2.4m)

**Goldfinch**
Multiflora rambler, 1907
Cupped flowers are golden-yellow with pronounced stamens. Relatively free of thorns. An ideal shorter rambler for northerly situations. 8 × 5ft (2.4 × 1.5m)

**Kathleen Harrop**
Bourbon, 1916
Very similar to 'Zéphirine Drouhin', the rose it sported from, but a softer pink. Thornless. Scented. Inclined to mildew. 10 × 6ft (3.0 × 1.8m)

### Kiftsgate
Filipes, rambler, 1954
A rose of huge proportions. It will cover almost anything. Masses of small, single, creamy-white flowers are borne in mid-summer and are followed by tiny red hips. 30 × 20ft (9.0 × 6.0m)

### Lady Waterlow
Hybrid Tea, 1903
The scented flowers of this rose are semi-double, soft pink with deeper shadings. A healthy plant. 12 × 8ft (3.7 × 2.4m)

### Mme Alfred Carrière
Noisette, 1879
Large, double flowers of white to blush pink have a tissue-paper-like quality and a beautiful scent. A vigorous rose with few thorns that produces flowers intermittently throughout the summer months. One of the best shade-tolerant climbers. 12 × 10ft (3.7 × 3.0m)

### Maigold
Pimpinellifolia hybrid, 1953
An early flowerer with large orangy-yellow flowers that are occasionally repeated later in the season. A vigorous grower with many tough prickles and excellent tough foliage. 12 × 8ft (3.7 × 2.4m)

### Mermaid
Bracteata, 1917
A very useful rose of large proportions. Single flowers are bright lemon-yellow with bold copper stamens produced throughout the whole of the summer. Excellent foliage, vicious thorns. 30 × 20ft (9.0 × 6.0m)

### New Dawn
Wichuraiana, 1930
Soft pink flowers are shapely and exude a delicious perfume. Foliage is glossy, dark green, and healthy. Will produce flowers well into the autumn. 10 × 8ft (3.0 × 2.4m)

### Paul's Lemon Pillar
Hybrid Tea, 1915
The scented blooms of this lovely rose are creamy-lemon and they will tolerate wet weather well. Summer flowering. 15 × 10ft (4.6 × 3.0m)

### Paul's Scarlet Climber
Multiflora, 1916
Medium-sized blooms are bright scarlet and loosely formed. Gives a good display only once each season, but still one of the best reds for shade. 10 × 8ft (3.0 × 2.4m)

### Rambling Rector
Multiflora rambler, of great age
Very popular and extremely vigorous. The semi-double flowers are creamy-white with a good display of golden anthers. This rambler is an excellent plant for covering nearly everything. 20 × 15ft (6.0 × 4.6m)

### Rosa multiflora 'Carnea'
Multiflora, 1804
Small pompon-like flowers are creamy-white tinged with blush pink. They are followed by bright hips in the autumn. 15 × 10ft (4.6 × 3.0m)

### Rosa multiflora 'Platyphylla'
Multiflora, 1816
Also known as 'The Seven Sisters Rose', it bears masses of medium-sized blooms that vary in colour on the same plant, from pale pink to almost red. Summer flowering. 20 × 10ft (6.0 × 3.0m)

### Souvenir du Docteur Jamain
Hybrid Perpetual, 1865
Probably the only Hybrid Perpetual really to tolerate north-facing conditions. The extremely dark red flowers have a powerful scent and, on a north wall, benefit from being away from scorching sunlight. This rose is relatively free of thorns, but it is inclined to mildew. Repeat flowering. 10 × 7ft (3.0 × 2.1m)

### Zéphirine Drouhin
Bourbon, 1869
A small climber that is completely thornless. When the flowers are at their best, their colour is almost shocking pink. Heavily scented, this is a good, late performer. 9 × 6ft (2.7 × 1.8m)

Other climbing and rambling roses suitable for north-facing situations are described and illustrated in the colour section. They are: 'Albéric Barbier' (page 106), 'Claire Jacquier' (page 64), 'Félicité et Perpétue' (page 56), 'Francis E. Lester' (page 109), 'Mme Caroline Testout' (page 68), 'Mme Grégoire Staechelin' (page 60), *Rosa mulliganii* (page 42), 'Shot Silk' (page 93), and 'The Garland' (page 44).

## FOR SHADED AREAS

### Aimée Vibert
Noisette, 1828
Pure white, double flowers are borne in nodding clusters on a relatively thorn-free plant. Very healthy with glossy foliage. 12 × 10ft (3.7 × 3.0m)

### Améthyste
Wichuraiana, 1911
Flowers, borne in clusters, are mauvy-crimson and fully double. Sends out vigorous, arching branches, well covered with polished leaves. 12 × 10ft (3.7 × 3.0m)

### Blush Rambler
Multiflora, 1903
Flowers of blush pink cascade in nodding trusses on an almost thorn-free plant. Abundant, light green foliage. 12 × 10ft (3.7 × 3.0m)

### Dr W. van Fleet
Wichuraiana, 1910
Semi-double flowers of gentle pink are perfumed and grace a well-foliated plant. Tolerant of most conditions. 15 × 10ft (4.6 × 3.0m)

### Ethel
Wichuraiana, 1912
Pink flowers overcast with mauve flounce in clusters on this vigorous rose. Glossy foliage, quite thorny. 20 × 15ft (6.0 × 4.6m)

### Mme d'Arblay
Multiflora, 1835
Fragrant flowers of blush-pink fading to white with age. The flowers are arranged in clusters on a vigorous plant with dark green foliage. 20 × 20ft (6.0 × 6.0m)

### Spectabilis
Sempervirens, *c*.1850
A shorter climbing rose that displays masses of pompon-like flowers in the summer, occasionally producing a repeat bloom in the autumn. Flowers are white, flushed with lilac and appear against dark green foliage. 8 × 6ft (2.4 × 1.8m)

### Splendens
Arvensis, 1835
Flowers semi-double, white cast with mauve, displayed in clusters. A vigorous rose with plentiful, glossy foliage. 20 × 10ft (6.0 × 3.0m)

### Vicomtesse Pierre du Fou
Hybrid Tea, 1923
Coppery-pink, scented flowers are semi-double and give more than one display each season. A healthy, vigorous rose with dark foliage that is sometimes tinged with the same copper shadings as the flowers. 15 × 10ft (4.6 × 3.0m)

Other climbing and rambling roses suitable for shaded areas are described and illustrated in the colour section. They are: 'Albéric Barbier' (page 106), 'Cécile Brunner' (page 62), 'Easlea's Golden Rambler' (page 94), 'Félicité et Perpétue' (page 56), 'Francis E. Lester' (page 109), 'Mme Caroline Testout' (page 68), 'Mme Grégoire Staechelin' (page 60), 'Paul's Himalayan Musk' (page 48), and 'The Garland' (page 44).

## FOR POOR SOILS

### Anemone Rose
Laevigata, 1895
Large, single flowers of silvery-pink with flushes of white around the edge. A thorny rose with glossy, light green foliage. Prefers a sunny position. Repeat flowering. 10 × 8ft (3.0 × 2.4m)

### Apple Blossom
Multiflora, 1896
From a distance this rose is aptly named but closer inspection reveals the flowers to be larger and more crinkled than those of the apple. Their mid-pink colouring fades with age to near-white. Foliage light green. Almost thornless. 10 × 6ft (3.0 × 1.8m)

### Cramoisi Supérieur
China, 1885
The climbing form of this rose does not flower as profusely as the bush, but it sometimes produces more than one crop of unfading, red flowers in a season. It seems to grow well even in the driest, hottest position. Foliage dark green. 12 × 8ft (3.7 × 2.4m)

### Cupid
Hybrid Tea, 1915
The large, single flowers – never produced in large quantities – are quite beautiful, a combination of pink and peach with bold, golden stamens. Summer flowering. 12 × 6ft (3.7 × 1.8m)

### Desprez à Fleur Jaune
Noisette, 1835
Fully double flowers are buff mixed with yellow and orange. They have a delicate scent. Foliage is light green. Repeat flowering. 20 × 10ft (6.0 × 3.0m)

### Gardenia
Wichuraiana, 1899
This beautiful rose deserves to regain popularity. It has large, slightly muddled creamy-coloured flowers with lemon flushes. The flowers have a lovely, fresh fragrance and they are beautiful against the background of very dark green, glossy leaves. 20 × 10ft (6.0 × 3.0m)

## Guinée
Hybrid Tea, 1938
Very dark red flowers made up of many velvety petals. They are scented and set off by dark leaves and stems. Sometimes repeats. 15 × 8ft (4.6 × 2.4m)

## Lady Hillingdon
See page 126.
The climber differs only in size. 15 × 8ft (4.6 × 2.4m)

## Leverkusen
Hybrid of *Rosa kordesii*, 1954
Lemon, semi-double flowers with a sweet perfume. These appear abundantly among healthy foliage all through the summer. 10 × 8ft (3.0 × 2.4m)

## Long John Silver
Setigera, 1934
Cupped flowers of pure white with a silky texture that catches the light to give this rose its silvery effect. Sweetly perfumed. Foliage large and leathery. 18 × 10ft (5.5 × 3.0m)

## Mme Sancy de Parabère
Boursault, 1874
This thornless climber with dark green foliage has beautiful, clear pink flowers with furled petals that appear in masses in mid-summer. Its foliage has a good autumn colouring. 15 × 10ft (4.6 × 3.0m)

## Meg
Hybrid Tea, 1954
A favourite rose of mine. The multi-coloured petals are mixtures of apricot, buff, and peach; they encircle very large, golden anthers. Flowers are scented and displayed against very dark green leaves. 8 × 4ft (2.4 × 1.2m)

## Ophelia
See page 128.

## Paul Transon
Wichuraiana, 1900
Double flowers are rich salmon-pink borne on a plant with an abundance of glossy, light green foliage. Prefers a sunny situation. 10 × 8ft (3.0 × 2.4m)

## Phyllis Bide
Multiflora, 1923
Flowers are basically apricot but with overtones of yellow and salmon. These continue well into the autumn and are set off by many small glossy leaves. 10 × 6ft (3.0 × 1.8m)

## Veilchenblau
Multiflora, 1909
A fast-growing rambler displaying trusses of violet to lavender flowers in mid-summer. These are sometimes flecked with white at the centre and fade to blue-grey with age. 15 × 12ft (4.6 × 3.7m)

## Wedding Day
Hybrid of *Rosa sinowilsonii*, 1950
A very rampant climbing rose bearing masses of medium-sized, single, white flowers. These have the added attraction of bold, golden anthers. Very glossy, bright green foliage. 30 × 15ft (9.0 × 4.6m)

Other climbing and rambling roses that tolerate poorer soil are described and illustrated in the colour section. They are: 'Albéric Barbier' (page 106), 'Albertine' (page 84), 'Alister Stella Gray' (page 53), 'Claire Jacquier' (page 64), 'Easlea's Golden Rambler' (page 94), 'Francis E. Lester' (page 109), 'Mme Caroline Testout' (page 68), 'Mme Grégoire Staechelin' (page 60), 'Paul's Himalayan Musk' (page 48), *Rosa mulliganii* (page 42), and 'The Garland' (page 44).

## FOR TREE CLIMBING

### Auguste Gervais
Wichuraiana, 1918
Semi-double flowers, buff-salmon at first, fading to creamy-white. Highly scented. Displayed to excellent effect against dark green, polished foliage. 12 × 8ft (3.7 × 2.4m)

### Chaplin's Pink
Wichuraiana 1928
Bright, blowsy, shocking pink flowers with bold stamens set off against glossy, mid-green leaves. 15 × 10ft (4.6 × 3.0m)

### Emily Gray
See page 131.

### Flora
Sempervirens, 1829
Soft pink flowers droop in clusters against dark green foliage and the plant is well suited to a smaller tree, such as an old, gnarled apple or pear. 12 × 8ft (3.7 × 2.4m)

### Kew Rambler
Soulieana, 1912
Small, single, pink flowers with white centres appear in masses in mid-summer and are followed in the autumn by small, orange hips. Very thorny growth helps it scramble into branches. 18 × 12ft (5.5 × 3.7m)

### Kiftsgate
Filipes, 1954
An extremely rampant and attractive rose (see page 132) – in the garden provide it with the largest tree possible.

### La Mortola
*brunonii* hybrid, 1936
Soft grey leaves provide the background for single, white blooms that, when fully open, are often dusted with pollen from golden anthers. This is a very vigorous, later flowering variety, its foliage lending it to the darker green of some conifers. 20 × 12ft (6.0 × 3.7m)

### Rosa gigantea
1889
The huge proportions of this species suit it to larger trees. Flowers are papery-white, wood is thorny, leaves dark green. Sometimes puts rather more energy into growing than producing flowers but, once established, is well worth the wait. 40 × 10ft (12.0 × 3.0m)

### Sanders' White
Wichuraiana, 1912
Many small, double, white flowers adorn a vigorous, wiry plant in mid-summer. These flowers are a pleasant foil against the dark, glossy leaves. Easily trained into a tree. 12 × 8ft (3.7 × 2.4m)

### Silver Moon
Laevigata, 1910
Large, single flowers of pure white set off by rich golden stamens. Occasionally repeats throughout the season but is always a little reluctant to flower in great profusion. 15 × 10ft (4.6 × 3.0m)

### Violette
Multiflora, 1921
Double, bright purple flowers displaying splashes of yellow from the stamens in their base. Quite vigorous, with few thorns. Good for the small or medium-sized tree. 15 × 10ft (4.6 × 3.0m)

### Wedding Day
See page 135.

Other roses that will do well as tree climbers are described and illustrated in the colour section. They are: 'Albéric Barbier' (see page 106), 'Albertine' (page 84), 'Alister Stella Gray' (page 53), 'Claire Jacquier' (page 64), 'Easlea's Golden Rambler' (page 94), 'Félicité et Perpétue' (page 56), 'Francis E. Lester' (page 109), 'Paul's Himalayan Musk' (page 48), *Rosa mulliganii* (page 42), and 'The Garland' (page 44).

## FOR GREENHOUSE AND CONSERVATORY

### Bouquet d'Or
Noisette, 1872
Flowers fully double and quartered, soft buff-salmon with a delicate fragrance. A vigorous rose that produces a continuity of flowers each season. 10 × 6ft (3.0 × 1.8m)

### Climbing Lady Sylvia
Hybrid Tea, 1933
This is another variety that grows successfully both outside and in. Its shapely flowers of soft pink are produced in large numbers and are delightfully scented. 15 × 10ft (4.6 × 3.0m)

### Crépuscule
Noisette, 1904
Double, blowsy flowers are apricot-yellow portrayed against light green leaves. Has few thorns and is repeat flowering. 12 × 5ft (3.7 × 1.5m)

### Devoniensis
Tea, 1838
Creamy-white flowers occasionally shaded pink. These are large and shapely and continue over a long season. Foliage is light green. Has few thorns of significance. 12 × 7ft (3.7 × 2.1m)

### Duchesse d'Auerstädt
Noisette, 1888
Flowers are a bold combination of apricot and gold with a pleasant perfume. They repeat throughout the season on a vigorous but not colossal plant. 10 × 8ft (3.0 × 2.4m)

### Gloire de Dijon
Tea, 1853
Although often grown out of doors with great success, this rose flourishes under glass. Fully double, buff-apricot, quartered flowers with a wonderful perfume. 12 × 8ft (3.7 × 2.4m)

### Maréchal Niel
Noisette, 1864
A tender rose that appreciates the warmer temperatures of a greenhouse. Scented, yellow flowers. Well foliated with large, mid-green leaves. 15 × 8ft (4.6 × 2.4m)

### Niphetos
Tea, 1889
Large, pointed buds of creamy-white open so loosely as to be paeony-like when fully open. Sweetly scented. 10 × 6ft (3.0 × 1.8m)

### Solfaterre
Tea, 1843
Large, double flowers of soft rich yellow. Can be outstanding under glass. Not averse to being grown in a large pot. 10 × 8ft (3.0 × 2.4m)

### Sombreuil
Tea, 1850
A climber of smallish proportions. Flowers are large, however, opening flat. Pure white with cream tinges at the base, exuding a pleasing scent. Repeat flowering. 8 × 5ft (2.4 × 1.5m)

## FOR THE SCENTED GARDEN

### Alida Lovett
Wichuraiana, 1905
Petals of peachy-pink with lemon flashes at their base. Perfume light and fruity. A healthy variety with very few thorns. 12 × 10ft (3.7 × 3.0m)

### Gardenia
See page 134.

### General MacArthur
Hybrid Tea, 1905
Blowsy blooms of ruby-red exuding a penetrating aroma. Vigorous with lush, dark foliage and beetroot-coloured wood. Rather thorny. 18 × 10ft (5.5 × 3.0m)

### Gloire de Dijon
See page 137.

### Guinée
See page 135.

### Lykkefund
Hybrid of *Rosa helenae*, 1930
Single, creamy-yellow flowers appear in massive clusters. Especially aromatic on warm summer evenings. Lots of good foliage and relatively free of thorns. 25 × 15ft (7.5 × 4.6m)

### Mme Abel Chatenay
Hybrid Tea, 1895
Soft pink flowers open from shapely, pointed buds to become large and full. Has an unusual, spicy perfume. Sometimes repeats. 10 × 8ft (3.0 × 2.4m)

### Paul's Lemon Pillar
See page 132.

Other climbers and ramblers that are to some degree scented are described and illustrated in the colour section. They are: 'Albertine' (page 84), 'Alister Stella Gray' (page 53), 'Claire Jacquier' (page 64), 'Francis E. Lester' (page 109), 'Mme Caroline Testout' (page 68), 'Paul's Himalayan Musk' (page 48), and 'The Garland' (page 44).

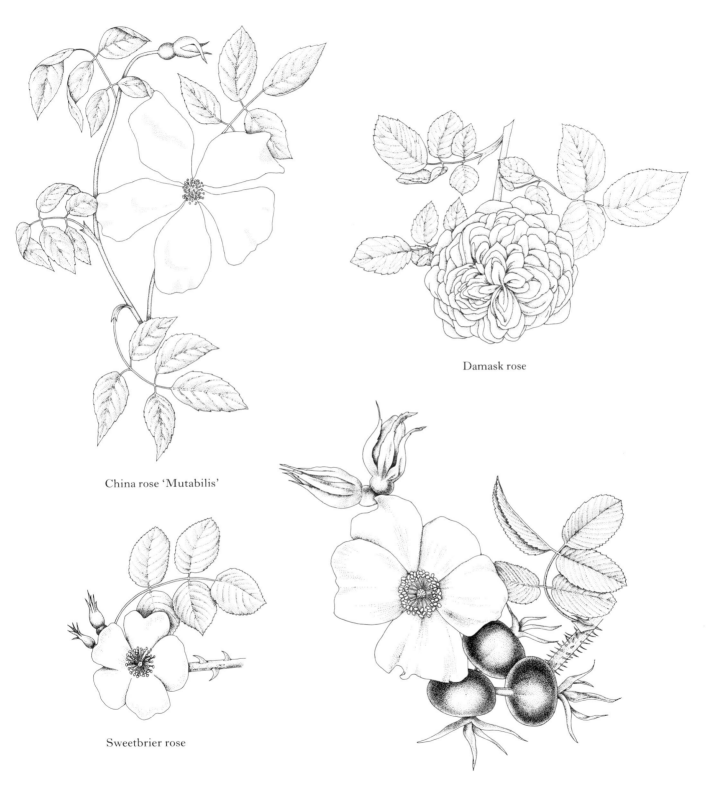

China rose 'Mutabilis'

Damask rose

Sweetbrier rose

Rugosa rose

# BIBLIOGRAPHY

Austin, David, *The Rose*, Antique Collectors' Club, Woodbridge, Suffolk, 1988

Beales, Peter, and Money, Keith, *Georgian and Regency Roses*, Jarrolds, Norwich, 1978
  *Early Victorian Roses*, Jarrolds, Norwich, 1978
  *Late Victorian Roses*, Jarrolds, Norwich, 1980
  *Edwardian Roses*, Jarrolds, Norwich, 1980

Beales, Peter, *Classic Roses*, Collins Harvill, London, 1985
  *Twentieth Century Roses*, Collins Harvill, London, 1988

Bean, W.J., *Trees and Shrubs Hardy in the British Isles* (8th edition), John Murray, London, 1980

Dobson, B. R., *Combined Rose List*, Beverly Dobson, Irvington, N.Y., 1987

Gault, S.M., and Synge, P.M., *The Dictionary Of Roses In Colour*, Michael Joseph and Ebury Press, London, 1971

Griffiths, Trevor, *My World Of Old Roses*, 2 vols, Whitcoulls, New Zealand, 1984, 1986

Harkness, J., *Roses*, Dent, London, 1978
  *The Makers Of Heavenly Roses*, Souvenir Press, London, 1985

Le Rougetel, Hazel, *A Heritage of Roses*, Unwin Hyman, London, 1988

Phillips, Roger, and Rix, Martyn, *Roses*, Pan Books, London, 1988

Warner, Christopher, *Climbing Roses*, Century Hutchinson, London/Globe Pequot Press, Connecticut, 1987

# GARDENS TO VISIT

## Great Britain

Castle Howard, near York, Yorkshire

Charlestone Manor, West Dean, West Sussex

Cliveden, Taplow, Maidenhead, Berkshire

Dixon Park, Belfast, Northern Ireland

Gardens of the Rose (Royal National Rose Society), Bone Hill, Chiswell Green, St Albans, Hertfordshire

Haddon Hall, Bakewell, Derbyshire

Hidcote Manor, Chipping Campden, Gloucestershire

Hillier Arboretum, Ampfield, near Winchester, Hampshire

Kiftsgate Court, Chipping Campden, Gloucestershire

Malleny House, Balerno, near Edinburgh

Mannington Hall, near Saxthorpe, Holt, Norfolk

Mottisfont Abbey, near Romsey, Hampshire

Nymans Garden, Handcross, near Haywards Heath, West Sussex

Oxford Botanic Gardens, Rose Lane, Oxford

Polesden Lacey, near Dorking, Surrey

Rosemoor Garden Charitable Trust, Great Torrington, Devon

Sheldon Manor, near Chippenham, Wiltshire

Sissinghurst Castle, near Cranbrook, Kent

Wisley Garden (Royal Horticultural Society), Woking, Surrey

Wolseley Park Gardens, Rugely, Staffordshire

## United States

American Rose Center, Shreveport, Louisiana

Berkley Rose Garden, California

Boerner Botanical Gardens, Hales Corner, Wisconsin

Brooklyn Botanic Garden, Brooklyn, New York

Columbus Park of Roses, Columbus, Ohio

Descanso Gardens, La Canada, California

Edisto Gardens, Orangeburg, South Carolina

Elizabeth Park Rose Garden, Hartford, Connecticut

E. de T. Bechtel Memorial Rose Garden, Botanical Gardens, New York

Exposition Park Rose Garden, Los Angeles, California

Hershey Rose Gardens and Arboretum, Pennsylvania

Huntington Rose Garden, San Marino, California

Idlewild Park, Reno, Nevada

International Rose Test Garden, Portland, Oregon

Lakeside Rose Garden, Fort Wayne, Indiana

Longwood Gardens, Kennett Square, Pennsylvania

Manito Gardens, Spokane, Washington

Maplewood Park Rose Garden, Rochester, New York

Missouri Botanic Gardens, St Louis, Missouri

Municipal Rose Garden, Kansas City, Missouri

Municipal Rose Garden, Oakland, California

Municipal Rose Garden, San Jose, California

Municipal Rose Garden, Tulsa, Oklahoma

Municipal Rose Garden, Tyler, Texas

Pageant of Roses Garden, Whittier, California

Queens Botanic Garden, Flushing, New York

Ritter Park Garden, Huntington, West Virginia

Rose and Test Garden, Topeka, Kansas

Roses of Legend & Romance Garden, Wooster, Ohio

Samuell-Grand Rose Garden, Dallas, Texas

Tennessee Botanical Gardens, Cheekwood, Nashville, Tennessee

# INDEX

Page numbers in *italics* refer to captions to the colour plates.